Software-Defined Networking with OpenFlow

Second Edition

Deliver innovative business solutions

Oswald Coker
Siamak Azodolmolky

BIRMINGHAM - MUMBAI

Software-Defined Networking with OpenFlow

Second Edition

First published: October 2013

Second edition: October 2017

Production reference: 1241017

Published by Packt Publishing Ltd.
Livery Place
35 Livery Street
Birmingham
B3 2PB, UK.
ISBN 978-1-78398-428-2

www.packtpub.com

Credits

About the Authors

Oswald Coker is currently serving as a partner at Crester Limited. Oswald has a Bachelor of Technology degree in information and communications engineering. He earned his Masters in Technology degree from the Vellore Institute of Technology. He is also a member of the Institute of Electrical and Electronic Engineers (IEEE) and other professional bodies. He has a number of scientific papers in international peer-reviewed journals and proceedings to his credit. Oswald is also a recipient of various awards. His current research interests are in various aspects of communications engineering, including (but not limited to): Software-Defined Networks, network virtualization, Internet of Things (IoT), and wireless (mobile) communications.

First and foremost, I would like to thank God for this opportunity. I would also like to express my gratitude to the Packt team, especially Sweeny Dias and Komal Karne for supporting me and working with me through this project. I would also like to express my gratitude to all the reviewers and editors; their comments made this book more valuable.

I would like to appreciate Tope Oyenuga and Professor Asha Jerlin who set me on the Software-Defined Networking path and Paul Zanna of Northbound Networks for his support.

My appreciation also goes to my friends and family for their support through this journey.

Siamak Azodolmolky received his computer engineering degree from Tehran University and his first MSc degree in computer architecture from Azad University in 1994 and 1998, respectively. He was employed by Data Processing Iran Co. (IBM in Iran) as a software developer, systems engineer, and senior R&D engineer during 1992-2001. He received his second MSc degree with distinction from Carnegie Mellon University in 2006. He joined Athens Information Technology (AIT) as a research scientist and software developer in 2007, while pursuing his PhD degree. In August 2010, he joined the High Performance Networks research group of the School of Computer Science and Electronic Engineering (CSEE) of the University of Essex as a senior research officer. He received his PhD (cum laude) from the Universitat Politécnica de Catalunya UPC in 2011. He has been the technical investigator of various national and EU-funded projects. Software-defined networking (SDN) has been one of his research interests since 2010, in which he has been investigating the extension of OpenFlow toward its application in core transport (optical) networks. He has published more than 50 scientific papers in international conferences, journals, and books. Currently, he is with Gesellschaft für Wissenschaftliche Datenverarbeitung mbH Göttingen (GWDG) as a senior researcher and has led SDN-related activities since September 2012. He is a professional member of ACM and a senior member of IEEE.

About the Reviewer

Jacob H. Cox Jr. received his BS in electrical engineering from Clemson University, SC, in 2002, his MS in electrical and computer engineering from Duke University, NC, in 2010, and his PhD in electrical and computer engineering from Georgia Institute of Technology, GA, in 2017. As an army officer with 21 years of active service, Jacob has served as a cyber officer, a telecommunications engineer, signal officer, and a chemical officer. His more recent assignments include company command at Fort Gordon, Georgia (2006-2008); assistant professor at the United States Military Academy (2010-2013), and Chief of Enterprise Operations at the South West Asia Cyber Center in Kuwait (2013-2014). More recently, Jacob accepted a position with Soar Technology, Inc. as a research scientist, where he plans to pursue his research interests in Software-Defined Networking, network control platforms, and network security.

www.PacktPub.com

For support files and downloads related to your book, please visit `www.PacktPub.com`. Did you know that Packt offers eBook versions of every book published, with PDF and ePub files available? You can upgrade to the eBook version at `www.PacktPub.com` and as a print book customer, you are entitled to a discount on the eBook copy. Get in touch with us at `service@packtpub.com` for more details. At `www.PacktPub.com`, you can also read a collection of free technical articles, sign up for a range of free newsletters and receive exclusive discounts and offers on Packt books and eBooks.

`https://www.packtpub.com/mapt`

Get the most in-demand software skills with Mapt. Mapt gives you full access to all Packt books and video courses, as well as industry-leading tools to help you plan your personal development and advance your career.

Why subscribe?

- Fully searchable across every book published by Packt
- Copy and paste, print, and bookmark content
- On demand and accessible via a web browser

Customer Feedback

Thanks for purchasing this Packt book. At Packt, quality is at the heart of our editorial process. To help us improve, please leave us an honest review on this book's Amazon page at https://www.amazon.com/dp/1783984287.

If you'd like to join our team of regular reviewers, you can e-mail us at customerreviews@packtpub.com. We award our regular reviewers with free eBooks and videos in exchange for their valuable feedback. Help us be relentless in improving our products!

Table of Contents

Preface 1

Chapter 1: Software-Defined Networks 7

  Understanding SDN 7

    Characteristics of SDN 8

      Plane decoupling 8

      Central control and simple forwarding elements 10

      Network automation and virtualization 10

  SDN use cases 11

    Data center applications 11

    Campus networks applications 12

    Service provider applications 12

    Mobile network applications 13

  NFV 13

    How is NFV different from SDN? 14

    NFV challenges 15

  Summary 15

Chapter 2: Introducing OpenFlow 17

  Activities around SDN/OpenFlow 17

  Building Blocks of an SDN deployment 18

    Header field 19

    Counters 21

    Actions 22

    Priority 25

    Timeouts 27

    Cookies 27

    Flags 28

  OpenFlow messages 28

    Controller-to-switch 29

      Features 29

      Configuration 30

      Modify-State 30

      Read-State 31

      Packet-out 32

      Barrier 32

      Role-Request 32

      Setting asynchronous configuration 33

Symmetric messages   33
   Hello   33
   Echo   33
   Errors   34
   Experimenter   34
Asynchronous messages   34
   Packet-in   34
   Flow-Removal   35
   Port-status   35
   Role-status   35
   Controller-status   36
   Table-status   36
   Request-forward   36
Northbound interface   36
Summary   37
Chapter 3: Implementing the OpenFlow Switch   39
OpenFlow reference switch   39
Controller-to-switch messages   41
Asynchronous messages   43
Symmetric messages   44
OpenFlow enabled switches   44
Software-based switches   45
Hardware-based switches   46
OpenFlow laboratory with Mininet   47
Getting started with Mininet   49
Experimenting with Mininet   57
Experimenting with Mininet GUI (MiniEdit)   61
   Getting started with MiniEdit   62
   Creating a custom topology on Mininet canvas   63
Configuring the controller   64
Configuring the switch   65
Configuring the host   66
Setting the MiniEdit preferences   66
   Saving the configuration   67
Running a Mininet topology simulation, generating logs, and monitoring
the flow table   69
Summary   71
Chapter 4: The OpenFlow Controllers   73
Software-Defined Networking controllers   73
Existing implementations   76
NOX and POX   77

Running a POX application   78
NodeFlow   85
Floodlight   88
    Virtual networking filter   89
    Firewall module   90
    Static flow pusher   91
    Network plugin for OpenStack   91
ODL   92
Ryu   92
Ryu architecture   93
    Ryu libraries   93
    OpenFlow protocol and controller   93
    Managers and core processes   94
    Northbound   94
    Applications   95
Installation of a Ryu controller   96
Running a Ryu application   96
Special controllers   98
Summary   99

Chapter 5: Setting Up the Environment   101
Understanding the OpenFlow laboratory   101
External controllers   105
Completing the OpenFlow laboratory   106
    Replacing ethX with the name of the unnumbered interface   108
ODL   110
ODL controller   110
ODL-based SDN laboratory   113
SDN Hub starter VM kit   117
Summary   119

Chapter 6: Net App Development   121
Net App 1 - an Ethernet learning switch   122
Building the learning switch   126
Net App 2 - a simple firewall   129
Net App 3 - simple forwarding in OpenDaylight   132
Net App 4 – simple switching hub using Ryu controller   135
Executing the Simple Switching Hub   138
Testing application   141
Net App 5 – simple router using Ryu controller   145
Creating the topology on Mininet   146
IP address configuration on the hosts   146

Configuring the default gateway on the host   147
Starting the Ryu controller   148
Configuring the address of the router (switch)   149
Configuring the default gateway of the switch   150
Verification   151
Conclusion   151
Net App 6 – simple firewall using Ryu controller   151
Creating the topology on Mininet   152
Starting the rest firewall application   152
Enabling the firewall   153
Creating rules   153
Verifying that these rules have been set   154
ICMP Verification   154
Configuring deny instructions   156
Conclusion   156
Summary   156
Chapter 7: Getting a Network Slice   157
Network virtualization   157
FlowVisor   159
Isolation mechanism   160
Bandwidth isolation   160
Topology isolation   161
Switch CPU isolation   161
New flow messages   161
Controller requests   162
Slow-path packet forwarding   162
Internal state keeping   162
Flowspace isolation   162
OpenFlow control isolation   163
FlowVisor API   163
FLOW_MATCH structure   165
Slice actions structure   166
FlowVisor slicing   166
Summary   173
Chapter 8: OpenFlow in Cloud Computing   175
OpenStack and Neutron   176
OpenStack Networking architecture   180
Neutron plugins   183
Summary   187
Chapter 9: Open Source Resources   189

Controllers 189
    Beacon 190
    Floodlight 191
    Maestro 193
    Trema 193
    FlowER 194
    Ryu 195
    Open Network Operating System 195
    Atrium 197
    OpenContrail 199
Miscellaneous 201
    FlowVisor 201
    Flowsim 202
    Avior 204
    RouteFlow 204
    OFlops and Cbench 206
    OSCARS 207
    Twister 207
    FortNOX 207
    Nettle 208
    Frenetic 208
    Open Exchange Software Suite 209
Summary 209

Chapter 10: The Future of SDN 211
    Packet forwarding innovations beyond OpenFlow 212
        POF 212
            POF architecture 212
            Structure of POFOX 214
            POFSwitch 215
        Programming protocol-independent packet processors 215
            P4 components 216
            Forwarding model of P4 216
    Protocol-independent forwarding 217
        Table Type Patterns 218
        Relationship between TTP and OF-PI 219
        Goals of OF-PI 220
    Optical transport protocol extensions 220
        Generalized Multiprotocol Label Switching 221
        Packet-optical Integration 222
    Summary 224

Preface

Decoupling network control from networking devices is the common denominator of Software-Defined Networking (SDN). SDN is a recent paradigm shift in computer networking, where network control functionality (also known as the control plane) is decoupled from data forwarding functionality (also known as the data plane), and furthermore, the split control is programmable. The migration of control logic, which used to be tightly integrated into networking devices (for example, Ethernet switches) into accessible and logically centralized controllers enables the underlying networking infrastructure to be abstracted from an application's point of view. This separation paves the way for a more flexible, programmable, vendor-agnostic, cost-effective, and innovative network architecture.

Besides the network abstraction, the SDN architecture will provide a set of APIs that simplify the implementation of common network services (for example, routing, multicast, security, access control, bandwidth management, traffic engineering, QoS, energy efficiency, and various forms of policy management). As a result, enterprises, network operators, and carriers gain unprecedented programmability, automation, and network control, enabling them to build highly scalable, flexible networks that readily adapt to changing business needs. OpenFlow is the first standard interface designed specifically for SDN, providing high-performance, granular traffic control across multiple networking devices.

This book looks at the fundamentals of OpenFlow, as one of the early implementations of the SDN concept. Starting from an SDN introduction, we will go from OpenFlow switches and controllers up to the development of OpenFlow-based network applications (Net Apps), network virtualization, OpenFlow in cloud computing, active OpenFlow-related open source projects, and the future of SDN. If you are still hungry for more, this book shows you how to set up SDN with OpenFlow.

What this book covers

Chapter 1, *Software-Defined Networks*, introduces you to the foundational topics that need to be covered before a deep dive into SDN and OpenFlow.

Chapter 2, *Introducing OpenFlow*, introduces OpenFlow, its role in the SDN ecosystem, and how it works in a computer network. This chapter shapes the required knowledge prior to the actual setup of an experimental environment. The notion of flow forwarding, OpenFlow functions, what OpenFlow tables can do, and features and limitations of OpenFlow have revisited again in this chapter.

Chapter 3, *Implementing the OpenFlow Switch*, covers the available implementations of OpenFlow switches, including hardware and software implementations.

Chapter 4, *The OpenFlow Controllers*, covers the role of OpenFlow controllers as a control entity for OpenFlow switches and the provided API (that is, northbound interface) for the development of OpenFlow-based network applications (Net Apps).

Chapter 5, *Setting Up the Environment*, introduces the options for OpenFlow switches and controllers. It also covers the environment for Net App development. This chapter focuses on the installation of virtual machines (VMs) and tools (for example, Mininet and Wireshark), which will be used in the next chapters for Net App development.

Chapter 6, *Net App Development*, covers developing sample network applications (for example, learning switch, firewall, and DHCP spoofing) to show how OpenFlow provides the common ground for Net App development.

Chapter 7, *Getting a Network Slice*, covers network slicing using OpenFlow and FlowVisor. A setup will be planned and the chapter will show how to configure and use a slice of the network using FlowVisor.

Chapter 8, *OpenFlow in Cloud Computing*, focuses on the role of OpenFlow in cloud computing and, in particular, the installation and configuration of OpenStack's Neutron. Neutron is an incubated OpenStack project that provides network connectivity as a service (NaaS) between interface devices (for example, vNICs or virtual network interface cards), which are managed by other OpenStack services.

Chapter 9, *Open Source Resources*, explains and gives pointers to the important open source projects that network engineers and/or administrators can utilize in their production environment. These projects range from controllers, virtualization tools, and orchestration tools to simulation and testing utilities.

Chapter 10, *SDN Future*, provides more insight into innovations expected to be introduced into SDN and OpenFlow.

What you need for this book

This book will guide you through the installation of all the tools that you need to follow the examples. You will need to install WebStorm version 10 to effectively run the code samples present in this book.

Who this book is for

This book is intended for web developers with no knowledge of WebStorm but who are experienced in JavaScript, Node.js, HTML, and CSS and reasonably familiar with frameworks such as AngularJS and Meteor.

Conventions

In this book, you will find a number of text styles that distinguish between different kinds of information. Here are some examples of these styles and an explanation of their meaning. Code words in text, database table names, folder names, filenames, file extensions, pathnames, dummy URLs, user input, and Twitter handles are shown as follows: "The message is OFPT_BARRIER_REQUEST and has no message body. " A block of code is set as follows:

```
if packet.dst not in self.macToPort:
        log.debug("Port for %s unknown -- flooding" %
        (packet.dst,))
          flood()
    else:
    port = self.macToPort[packet.dst]
```

When we wish to draw your attention to a particular part of a code block, the relevant lines or items are set in bold:

```
if packet.dst not in self.macToPort:
        log.debug("Port for %s unknown -- flooding" %
        (packet.dst,))
          flood()
    else:
    port = self.macToPort[packet.dst]
```

Any command-line input or output is written as follows:

```
git clone https://github.com/noxrepo/nox
```

New terms and **important words** are shown in bold. Words that you see on the screen, for example, in menus or dialog boxes, appear in the text like this: "Configure the VirtualBox for the **Host-Only Network Details** from **File** | **Preferences** | **Networks** | **Host-only Networks** | **DHCP Server**."

Warnings or important notes appear like this.

Tips and tricks appear like this.

Reader feedback

Feedback from our readers is always welcome. Let us know what you think about this book-what you liked or disliked. Reader feedback is important for us as it helps us develop titles that you will really get the most out of. To send us general feedback, simply e-mail feedback@packtpub.com, and mention the book's title in the subject of your message. If there is a topic that you have expertise in and you are interested in either writing or contributing to a book, see our author guide at www.packtpub.com/authors.

Customer support

Now that you are the proud owner of a Packt book, we have a number of things to help you to get the most from your purchase.

Downloading the example code

You can download the example code files for this book from your account at http://www.packtpub.com. If you purchased this book elsewhere, you can visit http://www.packtpub.com/support and register to have the files emailed directly to you. You can download the code files by following these steps:

1. Log in or register to our website using your email address and password.
2. Hover the mouse pointer on the **SUPPORT** tab at the top.
3. Click on **Code Downloads & Errata**.
4. Enter the name of the book in the **Search** box.

5. Select the book for which you're looking to download the code files.
6. Choose from the drop-down menu where you purchased this book from.
7. Click on **Code Download**.

Once the file is downloaded, please make sure that you unzip or extract the folder using the latest version of:

- WinRAR / 7-Zip for Windows
- Zipeg / iZip / UnRarX for Mac
- 7-Zip / PeaZip for Linux

The code bundle for the book is also hosted on GitHub at https://github.com/ PacktPublishing/-Software-Defined-Networking-with-OpenFlow. We also have other code bundles from our rich catalog of books and videos available at https://github.com/ PacktPublishing/. Check them out!

Downloading the color images of this book

We also provide you with a PDF file that has color images of the screenshots/diagrams used in this book. The color images will help you better understand the changes in the output. You can download this file from https://www.packtpub.com/sites/default/files/ downloads/SoftwareDefinedNetworkingwithOpenFlowSecondEdition_ColorImages.pdf.

Errata

Although we have taken every care to ensure the accuracy of our content, mistakes do happen. If you find a mistake in one of our books-maybe a mistake in the text or the code-we would be grateful if you could report this to us. By doing so, you can save other readers from frustration and help us improve subsequent versions of this book. If you find any errata, please report them by visiting http://www.packtpub.com/submit-errata, selecting your book, clicking on the **Errata Submission Form** link, and entering the details of your errata. Once your errata are verified, your submission will be accepted and the errata will be uploaded to our website or added to any list of existing errata under the Errata section of that title. To view the previously submitted errata, go to https://www.packtpub.com/ books/content/support and enter the name of the book in the search field. The required information will appear under the **Errata** section.

Piracy

Piracy of copyrighted material on the Internet is an ongoing problem across all media. At Packt, we take the protection of our copyright and licenses very seriously. If you come across any illegal copies of our works in any form on the Internet, please provide us with the location address or website name immediately so that we can pursue a remedy. Please contact us at copyright@packtpub.com with a link to the suspected pirated material. We appreciate your help in protecting our authors and our ability to bring you valuable content.

Questions

If you have a problem with any aspect of this book, you can contact us at questions@packtpub.com, and we will do our best to address the problem.

1
Software-Defined Networks

This chapter provides a solid foundation for **Software-Defined Networking (SDN)** concepts and other supporting technologies. Its characteristics are covered in this chapter as well as the various applications of SDN on production networks. Finally, **Network Function Virtualization (NFV)**, a concept often mixed up with SDN, is explored and the differences between SDN and NFV are explained in details.

In this chapter, we will cover the following topics:

- What is SDN?
- SDN use cases
- NFV

Understanding SDN

In a bid to understand SDN in relation with OpenFlow, it is necessary to provide a good background on SDN, its motivation, and what it promises. This chapter provides you with the required knowledge prior to the actual setup of SDN/OpenFlow, enabling experimental and developmental environments.

So what is SDN?

Traditional network technologies have existed from the inception of networking, even though various modifications have been made to the underlying architecture and devices (such as switches, routers, and firewalls) and frames and packets have been forwarded and routed using a similar approach resulting in limited efficiency and a high cost of maintenance. As a consequence of this, there was the need to evolve the techniques used in the architecture and operations of networks, which led to the birth of SDN.

SDN, often referred to as a revolutionary new idea in computer networking, promises to dramatically simplify network control and management and enable innovation through network programmability. Network engineers are responsible for configuring policies to respond to a wide range of network events and application scenarios. They manually transform these high-level policies into low-level configuration commands. These very complex tasks are often accomplished with access to very limited tools. Thus, network management control and performance tuning are quite challenging and error-prone tasks.

Another challenge is what network engineers and researchers refer to as internet ossification. Due to its huge deployment base and its impacts on different aspects of our life, the internet has become extremely difficult to evolve both in terms of its physical infrastructure as well as its protocols and performance. As emerging and demanding applications become more complex, the current status quo of the internet seems unable to evolve to address emerging challenges.

Present day network architecture is made up of a control plane, data plane, and management plane where the control and data planes are merged into a machine generally known as *inside the box*. To avoid these limitations, a new set of networks known as programmable networks have emerged, generally known as *out of the box*.

The main aim of SDN is to separate the control and data plane and transfer the network intelligence and state to the control plane. Some technologies that have exploited these concepts include **Routing Control Platform (RCP)**, **Secure Architecture for the Network Enterprise (SANE)**, and recently, Ethane. SDN is often related to the OpenFlow protocol. Currently, **Open Networking Foundation (ONF)** takes on the task of advancing SDN and standardizing OpenFlow, whose latest version is 1.5.0.

Characteristics of SDN

SDN can be recognized and distinguished from other innovative networking technologies by the features discussed in the upcoming sections.

Plane decoupling

Traditional network architecture comprises three distinct planes (control, data, and management), which enable full functionalities:

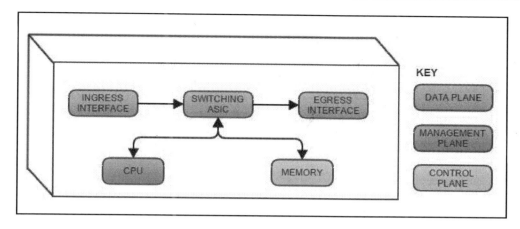

The main characteristics of SDN are the segregation of the control plane (which determines the way the traffic should be handled) and the data plane (which forwards the traffic based on decisions made by the control plane) based on incoming traffic parameters, such as the MAC address, IP address, and **Virtual Local Area Network (VLAN)** ID.

In SDN, these policies are determined by the control plane, which is decoupled from the switch (known as the forwarding element) to a logically centralized controller which can physically be distributed and communicated to the forwarding element via a secure link (OpenFlow channel):

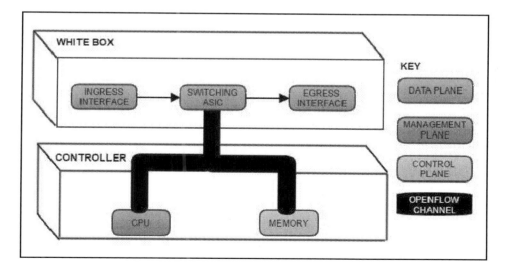

In the preceding diagram, the forwarding elements that will operate in SDN environments are designed to handle the data plane. The most predominant forwarding elements are designed to support traditional network architecture and SDN network architecture. Control and management plane functionalities are moved to a high-performance server that serves as the controller.

Central control and simple forwarding elements

Control and management plane hardware and software dedicated resources, which resided on the switches in traditional network architecture, have now been migrated to the controller. This new architecture presents a forwarding element, which maximizes the overall resource management in the topology as the hardware processes less complex codes for forwarding the traffic. These complex algorithms now exist in the controller, and traffic forwarding decisions are made from them, which communicates the best forwarding path for every packet to the forwarding element through a secure channel from the controller to the forwarding elements. These characteristics allow a simpler ASIC to be incorporated into the forwarding elements existing in an SDN infrastructure. This also allows the provisioning of ample resources with respect to the growth in the network size.

Network automation and virtualization

Network automation can be described as a process by which tools are deployed, which allows the automation of configuration, management, and operations of the network by the network administrator. As a result of this, the network administrator has the ability to tailor the network to fulfill the business requirement in real time. The SDN architecture better supports network automation in comparison to traditional network architecture.

Ansible and Puppet are common examples of automation and orchestration tools that assist network administrators with tasks ranging from the management of configuration to deployment of applications seamlessly. Automation makes the network flexible, resilient, easy to manage, and responsive to business needs in real time, which results in reduced operating expenses.

Network virtualization is the abstraction of the physical network to support the running of multiple network logical instances on a common shared physical element. This supports rapid innovation, as services can be at software speed across the entire network.

SDN controllers provide both automation and virtualization to the network by utilizing the northbound and southbound API to communicate with the applications and forwarding elements.

SDN use cases

Over the years, organizations have introduced SDN into their networks. SDN has been introduced because of its benefits, and the upcoming sections highlight the most prominent real-life applications of SDN in networks and how they have been adopted.

Data center applications

Data centers support traffic and applications that have diverse resource requirements ranging from high-bandwidth to security. The present day network architecture is rigid, which restricts the overall utilizable resource provided by the equipment in the data center. Considering the underlying principle of SDN, applications with specific needs can be deployed on an SDN infrastructure.

SDN can support multiple network instances on a single forwarding element, allowing maximum utilization of network resources, as shown in the following diagram. This feature supports the multi-tenancy requirement of future data centers:

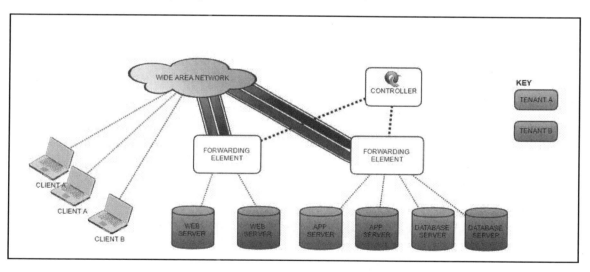

SDN also supports the micromanagement of the traffic traversing through the data center, as unique security policies can be assigned on the basis of the packet. Finally, with the rise of cloud-based applications, SDN supports the need for timely and dynamic allocation of redundant resources for maximum delivery of services per time.

Campus networks applications

Campus networks have evolved over the years with more complexity in technology and management introduced in them to support the growing user base. The initial architecture of campus networks was characterized by the finite number of nodes that were application-centric, such as firewalls and load balancers. Growth in the campus required a very complex network architecture, which could comprise hundreds of nodes.

In earlier campus network deployments based on traditional networks architectures, there existed a rigid foundation that required support for mobility, security, multiple devices, and variants of application packets. SDN comprises the best approach to tackle the ever-evolving networks present in campuses. For instance, campus networks require many policies considering the diversity of users present. SDN deployed with OpenFlow allows the provision of these policies across the network from the centralized controller.

SDN deployed on campus networks allows packet-level wide-visibility of traffic traversing through the network nodes per time. Network analytics grants the network administration access to analytics and thorough visibility of the network. In proactive network management, network administrators, upon reviewing analytics results, can deploy policies to maximize bandwidth allocation using the load balancer app existing in the north plane of the controller.

Service provider applications

Service providers have witnessed a high growth in the total user base in the last decade; the mobile growth rate of smartphone users, year on year, was approximately 12.1% from 2015 to 2016, which was a significant growth with respect to the infrastructure required to service the new users. SDN comes with a great potential to solve these issues faced by service providers.

The implementation of SDN for service providers comes with certain stringent requirements. SDN should be able to provide **high availability (HA)** and performance coupled with support for diverse forwarding elements as well as be able to accommodate various applications northbound of the controller. In addition, network virtualization should be supported in the SDN flavor used by service providers. Here, it is expected that the SDN architecture allows customers services (such as firewalls, **Intrusion Detection Systems (IDS)**, and **Virtual Private Networks (VPN)**) to be virtualized compared to traditional networks that require you to introduce middle appliance boxes.

Some service providers have been implementing SDN into their networks. AT&T, which is a pioneer, has seen benefits in the support of innovation, agility, and cost. AT&T program Domain 2.0 aims to control and virtualize 75% of its network using SDN methodologies by the year 2020. For more information, you can visit http://features.zdnet.com/huawei/huawei-the-carrier-challenge#transform-the-business. NTT communication has introduced SDN/OpenFlow solutions into its networks. Overcoming the 4000 VLAN limitation is one of the greatest benefits it can boast about.

Projections exist that service provider's investment in SDN and NFV will account for a revenue of over $18 billion over the years 2016-2020.

Mobile network applications

Mobile networks have been posed with various challenges over the years, which includes network flexibility and management. The management of the network has been a difficult task because of the diverse customer segments it supports and the **Operations Support Systems (OSS)** and billing support systems tools used for billing the subscriber.

SDN promises a significant boost in network management and flexibility because of the support for more granular traffic monitoring and dynamic bandwidth allocation. Network congestion, a critical challenge posed to a service provider, is addressed by SDN because the controller can optimize the various northbound apps in accordance to the network traffic in real time.

A striking advantage of the SDN implementation is multitenancy. It allows multiple mobile operators to utilize the same physical infrastructure. With SDN, this will be intelligently supported because the OpenFlow controller will support the application of granular policies to their traffic by multiple mobile operators.

NFV

NFV is the abstraction of the physical network to support the running of multiple network logical instances on a common, shared, and physical element. Network instances that are virtualized essentially function similarly to the equivalent physical instance.

A prominent example of network virtualization is VLAN. A VLAN is an abstraction of a physical switch in simple terms; it splits a single L2 broadcast domain into smaller logical domains that coexist without intercommunication between them. Communication between such domains requires the implementation of a layer three switch or a router.

Earlier implementations of network virtualization supported layer two (switching) and layer three (routing) services, but layer four to layer seven services such as firewalls and load balancers are now fully supported by network visualization.

Network virtualization maximizes the physical resources and ultimately grants full control, security, and efficiency to the network administration. It also cuts down the high cost of physical elements when compared to the virtual instances. The operational cost of elements such as cooling, power, and special requirements are cut down.

How is NFV different from SDN?

NFV is often mixed up with SDN. SDN is an approach introduced to bring intelligence into the network, while NFV is used to migrate network appliances such as IDS, VPN, and load balancers from the physical hardware to a virtualized platform.

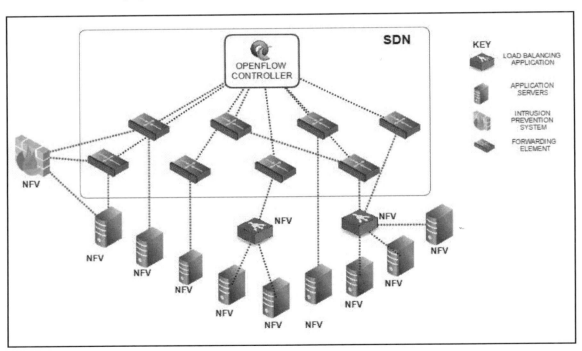

NFV technologies help cut down cost relatively but without an intelligent approach introduced to manage the virtualized resources. The overall operational cost remains the same because it suffers major constraints that physical hardware deployments suffer, such as manual management of policies.

SDN introduces automation in network infrastructures such that the virtualized services created by NFV can be more methodical and optimized for the maximum utilization of resources. The preceding diagram shows a pictorial view of SDN and NFV combined in a network.

NFV can exist fully without SDN, but SDN is the boost needed to reap the maximum benefit from NFV technology. Even though both technologies differ, combining them allows reduced capital and operational cost as well as optimized traffic flow across the network.

NFV challenges

NFV comes with some challenges that require considerations before implementing in existing networks. In large-scale networks, redundancy is a vital characteristic that is essential in order to minimize the downtime of the network if any network element goes down.

With NFV, the deployment should have redundancy at the physical level as well as the virtualized level. For instance, if the redundant switch is hosted on the same physical infrastructure, in the case of a power outage, both switches will fail, leading to a loss of connectivity.

Physical resources required to support a fully virtualized environment are limited. A physical host that supports multiple switch instances will require a network interface card of up to 100 Gbps for optimum functionality. The cost of such hardware to support a fully virtualized environment is on the high side.

Summary

In this chapter, we were able to create a good foundation, introducing SDN and its key characteristics. NFV was also explained in detail, and comparison between both technologies was covered. SDN applications were also covered, and we explained how they have led to a reduced total cost of operations in most large-scale network infrastructures. In the next chapter, we will cover OpenFlow in detail, along with its operation in an SDN infrastructure.

2
Introducing OpenFlow

This chapter introduces OpenFlow and its role in the SDN ecosystem and how it works in a computer network. It shapes the required knowledge prior to the actual setup of an experimental environment. The notion of flow forwarding, OpenFlow functions, what OpenFlow tables can do, and features and limitations of OpenFlow are recovered in this chapter.

We will cover the following topics:

- Activities around SDN/OpenFlow
- Building blocks of an SDN deployment
- OpenFlow messages
- The Northbound interface

Activities around SDN/OpenFlow

While OpenFlow has received a considerable amount of industry attention, it is worth mentioning that the idea of programmable networks and decoupled control plane (control logic) from data plane has been around for many years. The **Open Signaling (OPENSIG)** working group initiated a series of workshops in 1995 in order to make ATM, Internet, and mobile networks more open, extensible, and programmable. Motivated by these ideas, **Internet Engineering Task Force (IETF)** working group came up with **General Switch Management Protocol (GSMP)** to control a label switch. This group officially concluded and GSMPv3 was published in June 2002.

The active network initiative proposed the idea of a network infrastructure that would be programmable for customized services. However, the active network never gathered critical mass, mainly due to the practical security and performance concerns. Starting in 2004, the 4D project (http://www.cs.cmu.edu/~4D/) advocated a clean slate design that emphasized the separation between the routing decision logic and the protocols governing the interaction between network elements. The ideas in the 4D project provided direct inspiration for later works such as NOX (https://github.com/noxrepo/), which proposed an operating system for networks in the context of an OpenFlow-enabled network.

Later on, in 2006, the IETF **Network Configuration Protocol** (**NETCONF**) working group proposed NETCONF as a management protocol for modifying the configuration of network devices. The working group is currently active and the latest proposed standard was published in June 2011. The IETF **Forwarding and Control Element Separation** (**ForCES**) working group is leading a parallel approach to SDN. SDN and Open Networking Foundation share some common goals with ForCES. With ForCES, the internal network device architecture is redefined as the control element that is separated from the forwarding element, but the combined entity is still represented as a single network element to the outside world. The immediate predecessor to OpenFlow was Stanford's SANE/Ethane project (for more information, visit http://yuba.stanford.edu/sane/, and http://yuba.stanford.edu/ethane/), which, in 2006, defined a new network architecture for enterprise networks. Ethane's focus was on using a centralized controller to manage policy and security in a network.

A group of network operators, service providers, and vendors have recently created the Open Networking Foundation (https://www.opennetworking.org/), an industry-driven organization, to promote SDN and standardize the OpenFlow protocol. At the time of writing this, the latest specification of OpenFlow is version 1.5.1.

Building Blocks of an SDN deployment

The SDN switch (for instance, an OpenFlow switch), the SDN controller, and the interfaces are present in the controller for communication with forwarding devices, generally southbound interface (OpenFlow), and northbound interface (the network application interface), which are the fundamental building blocks of an SDN deployment. Switches in an SDN are often represented as basic forwarding hardware accessible via an open interface, as the control logic and algorithms are offloaded to a controller. OpenFlow switches come in two varieties: pure (OpenFlow-only) and hybrid (OpenFlow-enabled).

Pure OpenFlow switches have no legacy features or onboard control and completely rely on a controller for forwarding decisions. Hybrid switches support OpenFlow in addition to traditional operation and protocols. Most commercial switches available today are hybrids. An OpenFlow switch consists of a flow table, which performs packet lookup and forwarding. Each flow table in the switch holds a set of flow entries that consists of the following:

- Header fields or match fields, with information found in the packet header, ingress port, and metadata used to match incoming packets.
- Counters used to collect statistics for the particular flow, such as the number of received packets, the number of bytes, and the duration of the flow.
- Actions, which are sets of instructions or actions to be applied after a match, show how to handle matching packets. For instance, the action might be to forward a packet to a specified port.
- Priority, with information showing the precedence of the flow entry.
- Timeouts used by the switch to determine the maximum amount of time or idle time in which the flow should be discarded.
- Cookies, which are transparent data used by the controller to filter flow entries affected by flow statistics, flow modification, and flow deletion requests. It is not used in packet processing.
- Flags are used to alter the way flows get managed. For example, the CHECK_OVERLAP flag is used to inform the switch to verify that there is no conflicting flow existing on the switch with the same priority.

Header field

The decoupled system in SDN (and OpenFlow) can be compared to an application program and an operating system in a computing platform. In SDN, the controller (that is, the network operating system) provides a programmatic interface to the network, where applications can be written to perform the control and management of tasks and offer new functionalities. A layered view of this model is illustrated in the following diagram. This view assumes that the control is centralized and applications are written as if the network is a single system. While this simplifies policy enforcement and management tasks, the bindings must be closely maintained between the control and the network forwarding elements.

As shown in the following diagram, a controller that strives to act as a network operating system must implement at least two interfaces: a **SOUTHBOUND INTERFACE** (for example, OpenFlow) that allows switches to communicate with the controller and a **NORTHBOUND INTERFACE** that presents a programmable API to network control and high-level policy applications/services. **HEADER FIELDS** (match fields) are shown in the following figure. Each entry of the flow table contains a specific value, or any other value (* or wildcard, as depicted in the following diagram), which matches any value:

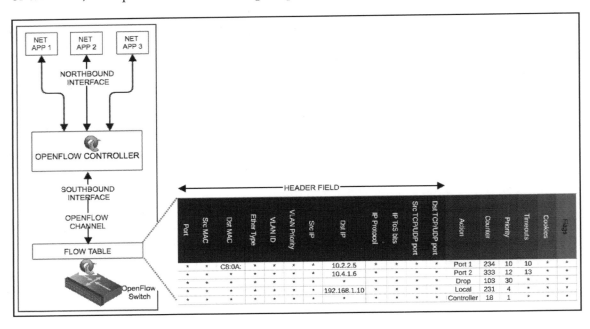

OpenFlow switch, Flow table, OpenFlow controller, and network applications

If the switch supports subnet masks on the IP source and/or destination fields, these can more precisely specify matches. The port field (or ingress port) numerically represents the incoming port of the switch and starts at 1. The length of this field is implementation-dependent. The ingress port field is applied to all packets. The source and destination MAC (Ethernet) addresses are applied to all packets on enabled ports of the switch, and their length is 48 bits. The Ethernet type field is 16-bits wide and is applicable to all the packets on enabled ports. An OpenFlow switch must match the type in both standard Ethernet and IEEE 802.2 with a **Subnetwork Access Protocol (SNAP)** header and **Organizationally Unique Identifier (OUI)** of 0x000000 (for more information, visit https://en.wikipedia. org/wiki/Organizationally_unique_identifier). The special value of 0x05FF is used to match all the 802.3 packets without SNAP headers. The VLAN ID is applicable to all packets with the Ethernet type of 0x8100.

The size of this field is 12 bits (that is, 4096 VLANs). The VLAN priority (or the VLAN PCP field) is 3-bits wide and is applicable to all packets of Ethernet type 0x8100. The IP source and destination address fields are 32-bit entities and are applicable to all IP and ARP packets. These fields can be masked with a subnet mask. The IP protocol field is applicable to all IP, IP over Ethernet, and ARP packets. Its length is 8 bits, and in case of ARP packets, only the lower 8 bits of the ARP opcode are used. The IP **Type of Service (ToS)** bits has a length of 6 bits and is applicable to all IP packets. It specifies an 8-bit value and places ToS in the upper 6 bits. The source and destination transport port addresses (or ICMP type/code) have a length of 16 bits and are applicable to all TCP, UDP, and ICMP packets. In case of the ICMP type/code, only the lower 8 bits are considered for matching.

Counters

Counters are maintained per table, per flow, per port, and per queue. Counters wrap around with no overflow indicator. The required set of counters is summarized in the following screenshot. The phrase byte in this screenshot (and throughout this book) refers to an 8 bit octet. Duration refers to the time the flow has been installed in the flow table of the switch.

The receive errors field includes all explicitly specified errors, including the frame, overrun, and CRC errors, plus any others:

Per Port			Per Meter		
Received Packets	64	Required	Flow Count	32	Optional
Transmitted Packets	64	Required	Input Packet Count	64	Optional
Received Bytes	64	Optional	Input Byte Count	64	Optional
Transmitted Bytes	64	Optional	Duration (seconds)	32	Required
Receive Drops	64	Optional	Duration (nanoseconds)	32	Optional
Transmit Drops	64	Optional	Per Flow Entry		
Receive Errors	64	Optional	Received Packets	64	Optional
Transmit Errors	64	Optional	Received Bytes	64	Optional
Receive Frame Alignment Errors	64	Optional	Duration (seconds)	32	Required
Receive Overrun Errors	64	Optional	Duration (nanoseconds)	32	Optional
Receive CRC Errors	64	Optional	Per Flow Table		
Collisions	64	Optional	Reference Count (active entries)	32	Required
Duration (seconds)	32	Required	Packet Lookups	64	Optional
Duration (nanoseconds)	32	Optional	Packet Matches	64	Optional
Per Meter Band			Per Group		
In Band Packet Count	64	Optional	Reference Count (flow entries)	32	Optional
In Band Byte Count	64	Optional	Packet Count	64	Optional
Per Queue			Byte Count	64	Optional
Transmit Packets	64	Required	Duration (seconds)	32	Required
Transmit Bytes	64	Optional	Duration (nanoseconds)	32	Optional
Transmit Overrun Errors	64	Optional	Per Group Bucket		
Duration (seconds)	32	Required	Packet Count	64	Optional
Duration (nanoseconds)	32	Optional	Byte Count	64	Optional

Required list of counters for use in statistical messages

Actions

Each flow entry is associated with zero or more actions that instruct the OpenFlow switch on how to handle matching packets. If no forward actions are present, the packet is dropped. Action lists must be processed in the specified order. However, there is no guaranteed packet output ordering within an individual port. For instance, two packets that are generated and destined to a single output port as part of the action processing may be arbitrarily reordered.

Pure OpenFlow switches support only the *Required Actions*, while hybrid OpenFlow switches may also support the **NORMAL** action. Either type of switches can also support the **FLOOD** action. The *Required Actions* are as follows:

- **Forward**: OpenFlow switches must support forwarding the packet to physical ports and the following virtual ones:
  - **ALL**: Sends the packet to all interfaces, excluding the incoming port
  - **CONTROLLER**: Encapsulates and sends the packet to the controller
  - **LOCAL**: Sends the packet to the local networking stack of the switch
  - **TABLE**: Performs the action in the flow table (only for the packet-out message)
  - **IN_PORT**: Sends the packet to the input port
- **Drop**: This indicates that all the matching packets should be dropped. A flow entry with no specified action is considered a Drop action.

The *Optional Actions* are as follows:

- **Forward**: A switch may optionally support the following virtual ports for forward action:
  - **NORMAL**: Process the packet using the traditional forwarding path supported by the switch (that is, traditional L2, VLAN, and/or L3 processing)
  - **FLOOD**: Flood the packet along the minimum spanning tree, not including the incoming interface.
  - **Enqueue**: This forwards a packet through a queue attached to a port. The forwarding behavior is dictated by the configuration of the queue and is used to provide the basic QoS support.
- **Modify field**: The optional (recommended) field modification actions are as follows:
  - Setting VLAN ID: If no VLAN is present, a new header is added with the specified VLAN ID (12-bit associated data) and a priority of zero. If a VLAN header already exists, the VLAN ID is replaced with the specified value.

- Setting VLAN priority: If no VLAN is present, a new header is added with the specified priority (3-bit associated data) and the VLAN ID of zero. If a VLAN ID header already exists, the priority field is replaced with the specified value.
- Striping the VLAN header: This strips the VLAN header, if present.
- Modifying the Ethernet source/destination MAC address: This replaces the existing Ethernet source/destination MAC address with the new value (specified as a 48-bits data).
- Modifying the IPv4 source/destination address: This replaces the existing IP source/destination address with a new value (associated with 32-bits data) and updates the IP checksum (and TCP/UDP checksum if applicable). This action is only applicable to IPv4 packets.
- Modifying the IPv4 ToS bits: This replaces the existing IP ToS field with the 6-bits associated data. This action is applicable only to IPv4 packets.
- Modifying the transport source/destination port: This replaces the existing TCP/UDP source/destination port with associated 16-bits data and updates the TCP/UDP checksum. This action is only applicable to TCP and UDP packets.

Upon a packet arriving at the OpenFlow switch, the packet header fields are extracted and matched against the matching fields' portion of the flow table entries. This matching starts at the first flow table entry and continues through subsequent flow table entries. If a matching entry is found, the switch applies the appropriate set of instructions associated with the matched flow entry. For each packet that matches a flow entry, the associated counters for that entry are updated. If the flow table look-up procedure does not result in a match, the action taken by the switch will depend on the instructions defined at the table-miss flow entry. The flow table must contain a table-miss entry in order to handle table misses. This particular entry specifies a set of actions to be performed when no match is found for an incoming packet. These actions include dropping the packet, sending the packet out on all interfaces, or forwarding the packet to the controller over the secure OpenFlow channel. Header fields used for the table lookup depend on the packet parameters as described as follows:

- Rules specifying an ingress port are matched against the physical port that received the packet
- The Ethernet headers as specified in the first figure and are used for all packets

- If the packet is a VLAN (Ethernet type 0x8100)), the VLAN ID and PCP fields are used in the lookup
- For IP packets (Ethernet type equal to 0x0800)), the lookup fields also include those in the IP header
- For IP packets that are TCP or UDP (IP protocol equal to 6 or 17), the lookup includes the transport ports
- For IP packets that are ICMP (IP protocol equal to 1), the lookup includes the **Type** and **Code** fields
- For IP packets with nonzero fragment offset or more fragment bit sets, the transport ports are set to zero for the lookup
- Optionally, for ARP packets (Ethernet type equal to 0x0806)), the lookup fields may also include the contained IP source and destination fields

Priority

Packets are matched against flow entries based on prioritization. An entry that specifies an exact match (that is, no wildcards) is always the highest priority. All wildcard entries have a priority associated with them. Higher priority entries must match before the lower priority ones. If multiple entries have the same priority, the switch is free to choose any ordering. Higher numbers have higher priorities. The following figure shows the packet flow in an OpenFlow switch. It is important to note that if a flow table field has a value of any (* or wildcard), it matches all the possible values in the header.

There are various Ethernet framing types (Ethernet II, 802.3 with or without SNAP, and so on). If the packet is an Ethernet II frame, the Ethernet type is handled in an expected way. If the packet is an 802.3 frame with a SNAP header and an OUI equal to 0x000000, the SNAP protocol ID is matched against the flow's Ethernet type. A flow entry that has specified an Ethernet Type of 0x05FF matches all Ethernet 802.2 frames without a SNAP header and those with SNAP headers that do not have an OUI of 0x000000.

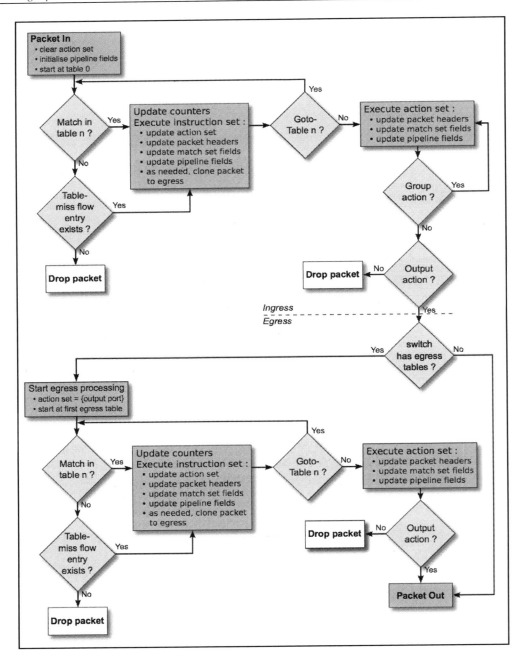

Packet flow in an OpenFlow switch

Timeouts

Timeouts in a flow entry are used to determine when a flow entry should be removed from the OpenFlow table. Timeouts in a flow entry could either be an idle timeout or a hard timeout. The idle timeout is a fixed value attached to a flow entry, which tells the switch to remove the entry if no packet hits the flow for a certain time. The hard timeout is a fixed value in which the flow is removed from the device irrespective of whether a packet hits a flow or not. If the timeout is nonzero, the switch takes note of the time of arrival of the flow entry in the scenario; it is required to be deleted in the future.

The hard and idle timeout ranges from the value from 0 to 65535. A syslog is always generated when a flow gets deleted due to either a hard or idle timeout.

The following table shows the behavior of a nonzero and zero idle and hard time outgoing:

Idle timeout	Hard timeout	Action
Nonzero value	Zero value	The flow compulsorily expires after the seconds set as the timeout elapses with no received traffic.
Zero value	Nonzero value	The flow entry is deleted once the hard timeout elapses, with or without a packet hitting the flow entry.
Nonzero value	Nonzero value	The flow entry will get deleted once the earlier idle timeout with no traffic or hard timeout seconds hits.
Zero value	Zero value	The flow entry is considered a permanent flow, which does not make it time out. Only a modification message, OFPFC_DELETE, removes it from the flow table.

Cookies

A cookie is a 64-bit value used by the controller, uninterpreted by the switch, which is used to modify and delete commands in the OFP_FLOW_MOD message. One of the applications of the cookie is to integrate the OpenFlow flow information with other flow export formats on the switch, such as NetFlow. Correlating these messages with the underlying flow proves to be difficult because of the conflict in the information generated from the message format or the use of wildcards. The problem is complex, considering it is almost impossible to synchronize with the flow table of the switch due to lack of reliability in flow expiration messages. Flow cookies make this correlation possible.

Another application is identifying a rule's source using flow cookies to gather statistics for access-lists hit count. An access-list defined in the controller may represent many OpenFlow rules. These access-lists contain OpenFlow rules, which can be tagged with a single flow cookie, making it easier to identify the source of an OpenFlow rule.

Flags

These are used to alter the way flows get managed. Flags are commonly used in various headers to specify certain actions; major ones include OFPXMT_OFB_TCP_FLAGS used in TCP header (EXT-109). This field is used to match all flags, such as SYN, ACK, and FIN, and can be used to detect the start and the end of TCP connections. Another common flag is OFPC_FRAG_REASM, which reassembles IP fragments before pipeline processing.

OpenFlow messages

The communication between the controller and switch happens using the OpenFlow protocol, where a set of defined messages can be exchanged between these entities over a secure channel. The secure channel is an interface that connects each OpenFlow switch to a controller. The **Transport Layer Security (TLS)** connection to the user-defined (otherwise fixed) controller is initiated by the switch with its power on. The controller's default TCP port is 6633. The switch and controller mutually authenticate by exchanging certificates signed by a site-specific private key. Each switch must be user-configurable, with one certificate for authenticating the controller (controller certificate) and the other for authenticating to the controller (switch certificate). Traffic to and from the secure channel is not checked against the flow table; therefore, the switch must identify incoming traffic as local before checking it against the flow table.

In case a switch loses contact with the controller as a result of an echo request timeout, TLS session timeout, or other disconnections, it should attempt to contact one or more backup controllers. If some number of attempts to contact a controller (zero or more) fails, the switch must enter the emergency mode and immediately reset the current TCP connection. Then, the matching process is dictated by the emergency flow table entries (marked with the emergency bit set). Emergency flow modified messages must have timeout value set to zero. Otherwise, the switch must refuse the addition and respond with an error message. All normal entries are deleted when entering the emergency mode. Upon connecting to a controller again, the emergency flow entries remain. The controller then has the option of deleting all the flow entries if it wants.

The first time a switch boots up, it is considered to be in emergency mode. The configuration of the default set of flow entries is outside the scope of the OpenFlow protocol.

The controller configures and manages the switch, receives events from the switch, and sends packets to the switch through this interface. Using the OpenFlow protocol, a remote controller can add, update, or delete flow entries from the switch's flow table. This can happen reactively (in response to a packet arrival) or proactively. The OpenFlow protocol can be viewed as one possible implementation of controller-switch interactions (southbound interface), as it defines the communication between the switching hardware and a network controller.

For security, OpenFlow 1.3.x provides optional support for encrypted TLS communication and a certificate exchange between the switches/controller(s); however, the exact implementation and certificate format is not currently specified. Also, fine-grained security options regarding scenarios with multiple controllers are outside the scope of the current specification, as there is no specific method to only grant partial access permissions to an authorized controller. The OpenFlow protocol defines three message types, each with multiple subtypes:

- Controller-to-switch
- Symmetric
- Asynchronous

Controller-to-switch

Controller-to-switch messages are initiated by the controller and used to directly manage or inspect the state of the switch. These type of messages may or may not require a response from the switch and are categorized into the subtypes discussed in the upcoming sections.

Features

Upon establishment of the TLS session (OpenFlow channel), the controller sends a feature request message to the switch. This message is used by the controller to know the basic capabilities of the switch as well as the identity of the switch.

Configuration

The controller is able to set and query configuration parameters in the switch. The switch only responds to a query from the controller.

Modify-State

These messages are sent by the controller to manage the state of the switches. They are used to add/delete or modify flow table entries or set switch port priorities. Flow table modification messages can have the following types:

- ADD: For ADD requests with the OFPFF_CHECK_OVERLAP flag set, the switch must first check for any overlapping flow entries. Two flow entries overlap if a single packet may match both, and both entries have the same priority. If an overlap conflict exists between an existing flow entry and the ADD request, the switch must refuse the addition and respond with ofp_error_msg with the OFPET_FLOW_MODE_FAILED error type and the OFPFMFC_OVERLAP error code. For the valid (non-overlapping) ADD requests, or those with no overlap checking flag set, the switch must insert the flow entry at the lowest numbered table entry for which the switch supports all wildcards set in the flow_match struct and for which the priority would be observed during the matching process. If a flow entry with identical header fields and priority already resides in a flow table, then that entry, including its counters, must be removed and the new flow entry must be added. If a switch cannot find any table entry to add the incoming flow entry, the switch should send ofp_error_msg with the OFPET_FLOW_MOD_FAILD type and the PFOFMFC_ALL_TABLES_FULL error code. If the action list in a flow modifies message references a port that will never be valid on a switch, the switch must return ofp_error_msg with the OFPET_BAD_ACTION type and the OFPBAC_BAD_OUT code. If the referenced port may be valid in the future (for example, when a line card is added to a chassis), the switch can either silently drop packets sent to the referenced port or immediately return an OFPBAC_BAD_PORT error and refuse the flow to modify the message.

- MODIFY: If a flow entry with identical header field does not reside in the flow table at the time the modify command arrives from the controller, the MODIFY command acts like an ADD command, and the new flow entry must be inserted with zeroed counters. Otherwise, the actions field is changed in the existing entry and its counters and idle timeout fields are left unchanged.

- DELETE: For delete requests, if no flow entry matches, no error is recorded and no flow table modification occurs. If a flow entry matches, the entry must be deleted, and then each normal entry with the OFPFF_SEND_FLOW_REM flag set should generate a flow removal message. Deleted emergency flow entries generate no flow removal messages. DELETE and DELETE_STRICT (refer to the next bullet point) commands can be optionally filtered by the output port. If the out_port field contains a value other than OFPP_NONE, it introduces a constraint when matching. This constraint is that the rule must contain an output action directed at that port. This field is ignored by the ADD, MODIFY, and MODIFY_STRICT messages.

- MODIFY and DELETE: These flow mode commands have corresponding _STRICT versions. In versions that are not RESTRICT, the wildcards are active and all flows that match the description are modified or removed. In _STRICT versions, all fields, including the wildcards and priority, are strictly matched against the entry and only an identical flow is modified or removed. For instance, if a message to remove entries is sent to the switch that has all wildcard flags set, the DELETE command would delete all flows from all tables. However, the DELETE_STRICT command would delete only a rule that applies to all packets at the specified priority. For the non-strict MODIFY and DELETE commands that contain wildcards, a match will occur when a flow entry exactly matches or is more specific than the description in the flow_mod command. For example, if a DELETE command says to delete all flows with a destination port of 80, then a flow entry that has all wildcards will not be deleted. However, a DELETE command that has all wildcards will delete an entry that matches all port 80 traffic.

Read-State

These messages are used to collect information from the switch. This information includes the running configuration, flow statistics, and capabilities. Read-State messages utilize the multipart message sequence for communication.

Packet-out

These are used by the controller to send packets out of a specified port on the switch as well as for the forwarding of packets received from any packet-in message. The buffer ID should be present for packets that are not complete and the list of actions, including the order in which they should be executed, must be applied to the packet for it to be forwarded.

Barrier

Barrier request/reply messages are used by the controller to ensure that message dependencies have been met or to receive notifications for completed operations.

Role-Request

In a network provided with multiple controllers for redundancy purpose, the roles of each controller are distinct and are assumed per time. The various roles that can be assumed by an OpenFlow controller include the following:

- **Master role**: In this role, the controller has complete access to all the switches. It executes commands such as `packet-out flow-mod`, `table-mod`, `port-mod`, which are capable of modifying the state of the switch by receiving asynchronous messages from the switch. Every other controller connected to the switch assumes the Slave role automatically.

- **Slave role**: Slave role is assumed by the controller when one of the peer controllers connected to the switch assumes the role of a master; commands capable of modifying the switch are not run by this controller. In the event that the switch receives such commands from a slave controller, it replies with an `OFPT_ERROR` message.

- **Equal role**: This is the default role assumed by all controllers connected to a switch, and it allows each controller to send asynchronous messages and commands to the switch.

Setting asynchronous configuration

Every OpenFlow channel conveys messages from the switch to various controllers present in the network. The controller manages its asynchronous configuration with the use of the OFPT_SET_ASYNC and OFPT_GET_ASYNC_REQUEST messages. The OFPT_SET_ASYNC message is used by the controller to determine whether it should receive any asynchronous message from the switch, while OFPT_GET_ASYNC_REQUEST is sent from the controller to the switch's reply message, OFPT_GET_ASYNC_REPLY, with the properties of the asynchronous configuration properties being sent to the controller in order to determine what is enabled.

Symmetric messages

Symmetric messages are initiated by either the switch or the controller and are sent without solicitation. There are four symmetric message subtypes in the OpenFlow protocol, as follows:

- Hello
- Echo
- Errors
- Experimenter

Hello

Hello messages are exchanged between the switch and controller upon connection setup. Version negotiation between the controller and the switch is necessary for communication to occur.

Echo

Echo request/reply messages can be sent from either the switch or the controller and must return an echo reply. These messages can be used to indicate the latency, bandwidth, and/or liveliness of a controller-switch connection (that is, a heartbeat).

Errors

The switch is able to notify the controller of problems using error messages.

Experimenter

This message is identified by the experimenter field and is used to create a new API and manage completely new objects. They are not attributed to any specific OpenFlow object.

Asynchronous messages

Asynchronous messages are initiated by the switch and are used to update the controller of network events and changes to the switch state. Switches send asynchronous messages to the controller in order to denote a packet arrival, switch state change, or an error. There are seven main asynchronous messages, as follows:

- Packet-in
- Flow-Removal
- Port-status
- Controller-status
- Table-status
- Request-forward

Packet-in

Packets sent to the controller from the datapath always utilize the `OFPT_PACKET_IN` message. For all packets that do not have a matching flow entry or if a packet matches an entry with a send-to-controller action, a packet-in message is sent to the controller. If the switch has sufficient memory to buffer packets that are sent to the controller, the packet-in message contains some fraction of the packet header (by default, 128 bytes) and a buffer ID to be used by the controller when it is ready for the switch to forward the packet. Switches that do not support internal buffering (or have run out of internal buffer space) set the buffer ID to `OFP_NO_BUFFER` and must send the full packet to the controller as part of the message.

Flow-Removal

When a flow entry is added to the switch by a flow modify message (the *Modify State* section), an idle timeout value indicates when the entry should be removed due to the lack of activity as well as a hard timeout value. The hard timeout value indicates when the entry should be removed regardless of the activity. The flow modify message also specifies whether the switch should send a flow removal message to the controller when the flow expires. Flow modify messages, which delete flow entries, may also cause flow removal messages. This is done by the data path with the OFPT_FLOW_REMOVED message.

Port-status

The switch is expected to send port-status messages to the controller as the port configuration state changes. This is done using the OFPT_PORT_STATUS message. The description field of the message signifies the action that has taken place by the port, 0 being ADD, 1 being DELETE, and 2 signifying some attributes of the port that has changed. An example of such events will include the change in port status (for example, disabled by the user) or a change in the port status, as specified by 802.1D (spanning tree). OpenFlow switches may optionally support 802.1D **Spanning Tree Protocol (STP)**.These switches are expected to process all 802.1D packets locally before performing flow lookup. Ports status, as specified by the STP, is then used to limit packets forwarded to the OFP_FLOOD port to only those ports along the spanning tree. Port changes as a result of the spanning tree are sent to the controller via the port-update messages. Note that forward actions that specify the outgoing port of OFP_ALL ignore the port status set by the STP. Packets received on the ports that are disabled by the STP must follow the normal flow table processing path.

Role-status

In the event that the role of a controller is modified by a switch, an OFPT_ROLE_STATUS message is sent to the controller in order to notify it of the change. Roles of the controller can be changed due to multiple reasons; these include another controller requested to be the master, change in configuration in the switch, and experimenter data being changed.

Controller-status

This message is generated when the status of the controller is changed; the switch updates all connected controllers with a controller status message that constitutes of the OpenFlow header, a controller status structure representing the current status of the changed controller with a reason code. There are several reasons the controller status could be reported. These include the controller requesting a status update, the operation status of the channel being changed, the controller obtaining a new role, a new controller being introduced into the network, a controller ID being changed, a controller being removed from the configuration, and experimenter data being changed.

Table-status

This is denoted by the `OFPT_TABLE_STATUS` message and is sent to the controller when there is a change in the table state. Change in the table state could be as a result of OpenFlow operations on the table or as a result of an internal processing capability of a switch.

Request-forward

This is used by a controller to notify other controllers about a modification in the state of groups and meters. It utilizes the `OFPT_REQUESTFORWARD` message. It should be noted that this is enabled on a per-controller basis.

 The heart of OpenFlow specification is the set of C structures used for OpenFlow protocol messages. Those of you interested in this can find these data structures and their detailed explanation available at `http://archive.openflow.org/documents/openflow-spec-v1.0.0.pdf`.

Northbound interface

External management systems or **network applications (Net Apps)** may wish to extract information about the underlying network or control an aspect of the network behavior or policy. Additionally, controllers may find it necessary to communicate with each other for a variety of reasons. For instance, an internal control application may need to reserve resources across multiple domains of control, or a primary controller may need to share policy information with a backup controller.

Unlike controller-switch communication (that is, the southbound interface), currently, there is no accepted standard for the northbound interface and they are more likely to be implemented on an **ad-hoc** basis for particular applications.

A potential reason is that the northbound interface is defined entirely in the software, while controller-switch interactions must enable the hardware implementation. If we consider the controller as a network operating system, then there should be a clearly defined interface by which applications can access the underlying hardware (switches), coexist, and interact with other applications and utilize system services (for example, topology discovery, forwarding, and so on), without requiring the application developer to know the implementation details of the controller (that is, the network operating system). While there are several controllers that exist, their application interfaces are still in the early stages and independent from each other and incompatible. Until a clear northbound interface standard emerges, SDN applications will continue to be developed in an **ad-hoc** fashion and the concept of flexible and portable Net Apps may have to wait for some time.

Summary

OpenFlow is the continuation of many previous efforts to provide decoupled control and data forwarding in networking equipment. A background of these efforts was presented in this chapter. Presenting the key building blocks of an SDN deployment, in particular, the OpenFlow protocol and its basic operation were covered in this chapter.

After introducing OpenFlow, in the next chapter, we present the reference implementation of OpenFlow switch in software and hardware, along with an introduction to the Mininet experiment environment.

3

Implementing the OpenFlow Switch

In this chapter, we will be covering the implementation of the OpenFlow switch (v1.0.0) and important hardware and software OpenFlow switches. Then, we introduce Mininet as an integrated environment to experience with the OpenFlow switches and controllers. The reference implementation of OpenFlow and hardware/software products will be presented in this chapter. An OpenFlow laboratory using Mininet network emulation is explained along with a step-by-step experiments in Mininet.

We will cover the following topics:

- The OpenFlow reference switch
- OpenFlow enabled switches
- OpenFlow laboratory with Mininet

OpenFlow reference switch

The OpenFlow switch is a basic forwarding element, which is accessible via the OpenFlow protocol and interface. Although this setup would appear to simplify the switching hardware at first glance, flow-based SDN architectures such as OpenFlow may require additional forwarding table entries, buffer space, and statistical counters that are not very easy to implement in traditional switches with **application specific ICs (ASICs)**.

In an OpenFlow network, switches come in two flavors: hybrid (OpenFlow enabled) and pure (OpenFlow only). Hybrid switches support OpenFlow in addition to traditional operation and protocols (L2/L3 switching). Pure OpenFlow switches have no legacy features or onboard control and completely rely on a controller for forwarding decisions.

Most of the currently available and commercial switches are hybrids. Since OpenFlow switches are controlled by an open interface (over TCP-based TLS session), it is important that this link remain available and secure. The OpenFlow protocol can be viewed as a possible implementation of SDN-based controller-switch interactions (which is a messaging protocol), as it defines the communication between the OpenFlow switch and an OpenFlow controller.

The reference implementation of OpenFlow switch from Stanford University includes `ofdatapath`, which implements the flow table in user space; `ofprotocol`, a program that implements the secure channel component of the reference switch; and `dpctl`, which is a tool for configuring the switch. This distribution includes some additional software as well (for instance, a controller, a simple controller program that connects to any number of OpenFlow switches, and a Wireshark dissector that can decode the OpenFlow protocol).

The following figure depicts the OpenFlow reference switch, interface, and three message types (controller-to-switch, asynchronous, and symmetric) and sub-types. These messages were briefly introduced in the previous chapter. They are presented with more implementation-related details in this section. Controller-to-switch messages are initiated by the controller and may or may not require a response from the OpenFlow switch.

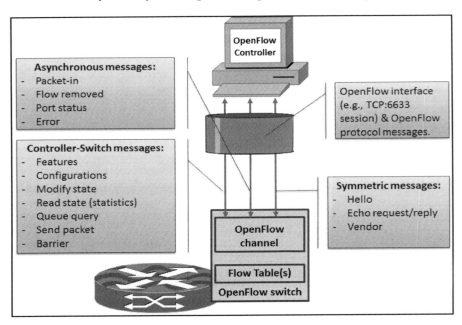

The OpenFlow interface and messaging protocol

Controller-to-switch messages

These messages are used to directly manage or inspect the state of the switch:

- **Handshake**: Upon the establishment of the TLS session (for example, the TLS TCP session on port 6633), the controller sends an OFPT_FEATURES_REQUEST message to the switch and the OpenFlow switch reports back (via the OFPT_FEATURES_REPLY message) the features and capabilities that it has and that it supports. The datapath_id field uniquely identifies an OpenFlow switch (datapath). It is a 64-bit entity and the lower 48 bits are intended for the switch MAC address, while the top 16 bits are up to the manufacturer. Datapath identifier (datapath_id) has a maximum number of packets the switch can buffer when sending packets to the controller using packet-in messages number of supported flow tables by data path (OpenFlow switch); switch capabilities, supported actions, and definition of ports are the important features that are reported to the controller. In the switch capabilities field, the OFPC_PORT_BLOCKED bit signifies that a switch protocol that is not OpenFlow, such as Spanning Tree, will detect and mitigate packet loops in the network.

- **Switch configuration**: The controller is able to set and query configuration parameters in the switch with the OFPT_SET_CONFIG and OFPT_GET_CONFIG_REPLY messages, respectively. The switch responds to a configuration request with an OFPT_GET_CONFIG_REPLY message; it does not reply to a request to set the configuration. In OFPT_GET_CONFIG_REPLY, the only content is the OpenFlow header that contains two major contents:

    - The flag that is used to indicate whether the IP fragment should be treated normally, dropped, or reassembled. Normal handling of a fragment is mandatory for an OpenFlow switch, and it kicks in when a fragment misses any perquisite field, such as the TCP/UDP port; in such a scenario, the packet should not match any entry that has that field set.

    - The miss_send_len field defines the number of bytes sent to the controller by the OpenFlow pipeline when an output action is not used to the OFP_CONTROLLER logical port. An instance can be when a packet has an invalid TTL sent; with this field set as 0, the switch must send zero bytes of the packet in the ofp_packet_in message, and if the value is set to OFPCL_NO_BUFFER, the complete packet must be included in the message and should not be buffered.

- **Flow table configuration**: This is used by the switch to determine which tables the configuration should be applied to. The table numbering is from 0 and can take any number until OFPTT_MAX. OFPTT_ALL is a reserved value used when the configuration is to be applied to all the tables in the switch.

- **Modify state**: Modifications to the flow table from the controller are done with the OFPT_FLOW_MOD message, and the controller uses the OFPT_PORT_MOD message to modify the behavior of the physical ports. The flow modification commands are ADD, MODIFY, MODIFY_STRICT, DELETE, and DELETE_STRICT, which were explained in Chapter 2, *Introducing OpenFlow*. The port configuration bits indicate whether a port has been administratively brought down, the options for handling 802.1D **Spanning Tree Protocol (STP)** packets, and how to handle incoming and outgoing packets. The controller may set OFPPFL_NO_STP to 0 to enable STP on a port or to 1 in order to disable STP on a port. The OpenFlow reference implementation sets this bit to 0 (enabling STP) by default.

- **Read State (Statistics)**: The controller can query the status of the switch using the OFPT_STAT_REQUEST message. The switch responds with one or more OFPT_STATS_REPLY messages. There is a type field in these message exchange, which specifies the kind of information that are begin exchanged (OpenFlow switch description, individual flow statistics, aggregate flow statistics, flow table statistics, physical port statistics, queue statistics for a port, and vendor-specific messages) and determines how the body field should be interpreted.

- **Queue query**: An OpenFlow switch provides limited **Quality of Service (QoS)** support through a simple queuing mechanism. One (or more) queue(s) can be attached to a port and can be used to map flows on it (them). The flows, which are mapped to a specific queue, will be treated according to the configuration of that queue (for example, the minimum rate control). Note that queue configuration takes place outside the OpenFlow protocol (for example, through the command-line interface) or an external dedicated configuration protocol. The controller can query the switch for configured queues on a port using the queue query message.

- **Send packet**: Using this message (that is, OFPT_PACKET_OUT), the controller is able to send packets out of a specified port of the OpenFlow switch.

- **Barrier**: This message is sent whenever the controller wants to ensure message dependencies have been met or wants to receive notifications for completed operations. The message is OFPT_BARRIER_REQUEST and has no message body. Upon receipt, the OpenFlow switch must finish processing all previously received messages before executing any message beyond the barrier request. When current processing is completed, the switch must send an OFPT_BARRIER_REPLY message the transaction ID (xid) of the original request.

Asynchronous messages

Asynchronous messages are initiated by the switch and are used to update the controller of network events and changes to the switch state. Switches send asynchronous messages to the controller in order to denote a packet arrival, flow removal, port status change, or an error.

- **Packet-in**: This is used when packets are received by the switch (data path) and are sent to the controller using the OFPT_PACKET_IN message. When a packet is buffered in the switch, some number of bytes from the message will be included in the data portion of the message. If the packet is sent because of a send-to-controller action, then max_len bytes are sent, and if the packet is sent due to a flow table miss, then at least miss_send_len bytes are sent. If the packet is not buffered inside the switch, then the entire packet is included in the data portion of the message. Switches that implement buffering are expected to expose the amount of buffering and the length of time before buffers may be reused. An OpenFlow switch must gracefully handle cases where a buffered packet_in message gets no response from the controller.
- **Flow-Removed**: When flows times out, the OpenFlow switch notifies the controller with the OFPT_FLOW_REMOVED message (if the controller has requested to be notified). The duration_sec and duration_nsec fields of the message indicate the elapsed time for which the flow has been installed in the switch. The total duration, in nanoseconds, can be computed as duration_sec x 109 + duration_nsec. Implementations are required to provide millisecond precision. The idle_timeout field is directly extracted from the FLOW_MOD that created the flow table entry.

- **Port-Status**: As physical ports are added, modified, and possibly removed from the data path, the controller needs to be informed with the OPFT_PORT_STATUS message. Also, there are cases where the OpenFlow switch needs to notify the controller of a problem. The message includes an error type, error code, and variable-length data that should be interpreted according to the error type and code. In most cases, the data part is the message that caused the problem. There are six types of error. OFPET_HELLO_FAILED indicates that the HELLO protocol failed. OFPET_BAD_REQUEST refers to the case where the request was not understood. Error in action description is indicated by OFPET_BAD_ACTION. If the FLOW_MOD or PORT_MOD requests are failed, then the error type is OFPET_FLOW_MOD_FAILED and OFPET_PORT_MOD_FAILED, respectively. Failure in port queue operations is classified with OFPET_QUEUE_OP_FAILED.

Symmetric messages

Symmetric messages are sent in any direction without any solicitation. There are four messages that exist here: the hello, echo, error, and experimenter messages.

The hello message (OFPT_HELLO), echo request/reply, and vendor message are symmetric OpenFlow messages. In the OpenFlow reference implementation that includes a user space process and a kernel module, echo request/reply is implemented in the kernel module. This implementation consideration provides more accurate end-to-end latency timing. The vendor field in the OFPT_VENDOR message is a 32-bit value that uniquely identifies the vendor. If the most significant byte is zero, the next three bytes (24 bits) are the vendor's IEEE OUI. If a switch does not understand a vendor extension, it must send an OFPT_ERROR message with an OFPET_BAD_REQUEST error type and an OFPBRC_BAD_VENDOR error code.

OpenFlow enabled switches

OpenFlow reference standard (OpenFlow 1.5.1, wire protocol 0x06) is the latest SDN enabling technology currently being implemented in the commodity-networking hardware. In this section, we do not intend to provide a complete detailed overview of OpenFlow enabled switches and manufacturers but rather a brief list of a few options that are cost-effective and available in the market. These switches can be divided into two versions.

Software-based switches

Software-based switches are more frequently used in test environments to run an OpenFlow test-bed or to develop and test OpenFlow-based network application. There are currently several OpenFlow software switches that can be used, some of which are listed with a brief description, including the implementation language and the OpenFlow standard, as follows:

- **Open vSwitch**: Open vSwitch is a multilayer and production quality virtual switch licensed under the Apache 2.0 license. It is designed to enable network automation through programmatic extension while still supporting standard management interfaces and protocols (for example, NetFlow, sFlow, IPFIX, RSPAN, **command-line interface (CLI)**, LACP, 802.1ag, OpenFlow, OVSDB, and so on).

- **Pantou (OpenWRT)**: Pantou (OpenWRT) turns a commercial wireless router/access point to an OpenFlow-enabled switch. OpenFlow is implemented as an application on top of OpenWRT. Pantou is based on the BackFire OpenWrt release (Linux 2.6.32). The OpenFlow module is based on the Stanford reference implementation (userspace). At the time of writing this, it supports generic Broadcom (BRCM43xx Wi-Fi) and some models of LinkSys and TP-LINK (WR1043ND) access points with Broadcom (BRCM47xx/953XX) and Atheros (AR71xx) chipsets.

- **Indigo**: Indigo first generation is an open source OpenFlow implementation that runs on physical switches and uses the hardware features of Ethernet switch ASICs to run OpenFlow at line rates. It is based on the OpenFlow reference implementation of the Stanford University. **Indigo Virtual Switch (IVS)**, based on the Indigo Framework was introduced, which is an open source virtual switch for Linux compatible with the KVM hypervisor and that leverages the Open vSwitch kernel module for packet forwarding. It is a lightweight, high-performance vSwitch built from the ground up to support the OpenFlow protocol. It is designed to enable high-scale network virtualization applications and supports distribution across multiple physical servers using an OpenFlow enabled controller, similar to VMware's vNetwork, Cisco's Nexus or Open vSwitch.

- **LINC**: LINC is an open source project led by FlowForwarding effort and is an Apache 2 license implementation based on OpenFlow 1.2/1.3.1. LINC is architected to use generally available commodity x86 hardware and runs on a variety of platforms such as Linux, Solaris, Windows, macOS, and FreeBSD, where the Erlang runtime is available. The benefit of the x86-based platform is that LINC can take advantage of the availability of lots of CPU cores and memory and scale gracefully to increase and decrease compute resources. This is critical when many logical switches are instantiated on a single OpenFlow capable switch.

- **Xorplus**: Xorplus is a switching software provided by Pica8 and supported by the open community. It provides no-cost Layer 2/Layer 3 protocol stacks, enabling the community to innovate. It supports protocols such as PIM-SM, IGMP, IGMP snooping, VRRP, IPFIX, and SNMP. It also powers Pica8's current pronto line of switches.

- **Of13softswitch**: Of13softswitch is an OpenFlow 1.3 compatible user-space software switch implementation based on the Ericsson TrafficLab 1.1 softswitch. The latest version of this software switch includes the switch implementation (`ofdatapath`), the secure channel for connecting the switch to the controller (`ofprotocol`), a library for conversion from/to OpenFlow 1.3 (`oflib`), and a configuration tool (`dpctl`). This project is supported by Ericsson Innovation Center in Brazil and maintained by CPqD in technical collaboration with Ericsson Research.

Hardware-based switches

- **Zodiac FX**: The Zodiac FX is the world's smallest and most affordable OpenFlow enabled switch. It provides many of the features of an enterprise-grade switch; yet, it's small enough to fit in the palm of your hand, making it perfect for research and education. It currently supports OpenFlow version 1.0 and version 1.3.

- **Pica8 (P3297, P3930)**: Pica8's open switches are ideal for cloud or virtualized data centers that require flexibility and adaptability. These switches seamlessly integrate with today's data center applications on traditional network architectures, while allowing the exploration of new **Software-Defined Networking (SDN)** technologies, such as OpenFlow. Pica8 white box switches run PicOS™, an open network OS that runs standards-based Layer 2/Layer 3 protocols with industry-leading OpenFlow 1.4/Open vSwitch (OVS) 2.0 integration.

OVS runs as a process within PicOS and provides the OpenFlow interface for external programmability. PicOS utilizes proven high-performance hardware with a switching fabric capacity of 1.28 Tbps and options for 10 GbE copper and fiber connectivity.

- **Hewlett Packard 2920**: The HP 2920 Switch Series consists of four switches: the HP 2920-24G and 2920-24G-PoE+ switches with 24 10/100/1000 ports and the HP 2920-48G and 2920-48G-PoE+ switches with 48 10/100/1000 ports. Each switch has four dual-personality ports for 10/100/1000 or SFP connectivity. These switches support traditional technologies coupled with OpenFlow® support for SDN. The 2920 series of switches are most suitable for high-performance networks present in enterprise networks.
- **IBM Programmable Network Controller**: The IBM Programmable Network Controller provides an OpenFlow-based fabric with centralized control of network flows and unlimited **virtual machine** (**VM**) mobility implemented in enterprise-class software. The controller automatically discovers the OpenFlow topology and maps physical and virtual traffic flows across any OpenFlow-based data center network environment. The IBM PNC helps provide a highly reliable, edge-to-edge system network fabric that can be defined for multi-tenant environments. Granular policy enforcements ensure isolation across multiple tenants. Administrators can use the IBM PNC to attach policies that direct overall network operations.

OpenFlow laboratory with Mininet

Mininet is a software tool that allows an entire OpenFlow network to be emulated on a single computer. Mininet uses lightweight process-based virtualization (Linux network namespaces and Linux container architecture) to run many hosts and switches (for instance, 4096) on a single OS kernel. It can create kernel or user-space OpenFlow switches, controllers to control the switches, and hosts to communicate over the emulated network.

Mininet connects switches and hosts using **virtual ethernet** (**veth**) pairs. It considerably simplifies the initial development, debugging, testing, and deployment process. New network applications can be first developed and tested on an emulation of the anticipated deployment network. It can then be moved to the actual operational infrastructure. Mininet currently depends on the Linux kernel; future deployments may support process-based virtualization on other OS. By default, Mininet supports OpenFlow v1.0.

However, it may be modified to support a software switch that implements a newer release. Some of the key features and benefits of Mininet are as follows:

- Mininet creates a network of virtual hosts, switches, controllers, and links.
- Mininet hosts run standard Linux network software, and its switches support OpenFlow. It can be considered an inexpensive OpenFlow laboratory for developing OpenFlow applications. It enables complex topology testing, without the need to wire up a physical network.
- Mininet enables multiple concurrent developers to work independently on the same topology.
- It also supports system-level regression tests, which are repeatable and easily packaged.
- Mininet includes a CLI that is topology-aware and OpenFlow-aware for debugging or running network-wide tests.
- You can start using Mininet out of the box without any programming, but it also provides a straightforward and extensible Python API for network creation and experimentation.
- Instead of being a simulation tool, Mininet is an emulation environment, which runs real, unmodified code including application code, OS kernel code, and control plane code (both OpenFlow controller code and Open vSwitch code).
- Designs implemented can be deployed on a real system for real-world testing, performance evaluation, and deployment because Mininet networks run real codes, including Linux network applications.
- It is easy to install and available as a prepackaged VM image that runs on VMware or VirtualBox for Mac/Windows/Linux with OpenFlow v1.0 tools already installed.

In the rest of this section, we provide a tutorial overview of Mininet, which will be also used in the rest of this book.

Getting started with Mininet

The easiest way to get started with Mininet is to download a prepackaged VM image of Mininet (which runs over Ubuntu). This VM includes all OpenFlow binaries and preinstalled tools to support large Mininet networks along with Mininet itself. In addition to prepackaged VM installation, those of you interested can install it natively from the source code or packages on Ubuntu.

 The examples in this chapter are based on Version 2.2 of Mininet. The latest version of Mininet can be downloaded from http://mininet.org/download/.

If you want to get the VM image, you have to download and install a virtualization system. VirtualBox (free, GPL) or VMware Player (free for non-commercial use) are the available choices, which are free and work on Windows, macOS, and Linux. Mininet is an **Open Virtualization Format** (**OVF**) image file (approximately 1 GB), which can be imported by VirtualBox or VMware Player (free for non-commercial use).

In VirtualBox, you can import the Mininet's OVF file by double-clicking on the VM image or going to **File** and selecting **Import Appliance**. Then, go to **Settings** and add an additional host-only network adapter to log in to the VM image. If you are using VMware, it may ask you to install VMware tools on the VM; if it asks, decline. In the following examples, we have used VirtualBox as our virtualization system for Mininet.

Here, are the steps are shown pictorially.

To reach the same environment, you can take the following steps:

1. Download and install Xming X-Server, Putty (with X11 forwarding option enabled) and VirtualBox. The X11 forwarding (refer to the following information box for more information) enables you to execute programs with a graphical output (for example, Wireshark, which is preinstalled and included in the Mininet VM image).

2. Set up the networking preference of the VirtualBox, shown as follows:

1. Enable the second adapter on the VirtualBox, go to **Preferences** | **Network** | **Host-only Networks**. Accessing the preferences tab can be done using the *Ctrl + G* shortcut. Ensure the configuration match with the following screenshot:
   - The DHCP server is enabled
   - The address space matches what is in the diagram

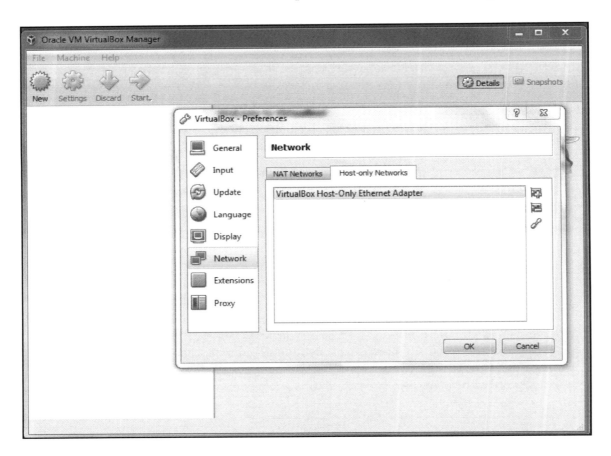

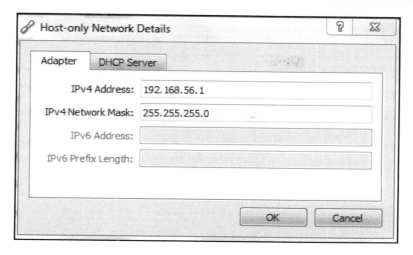

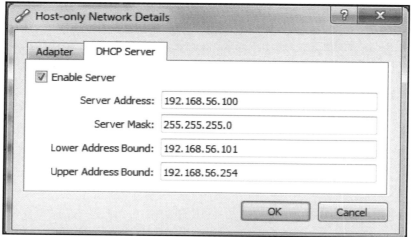

2. Import the extracted downloaded Mininet appliance:

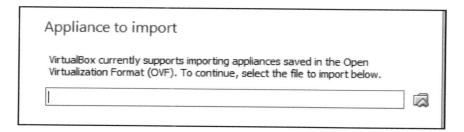

3. Configure the Putty to enable X11 forwarding:

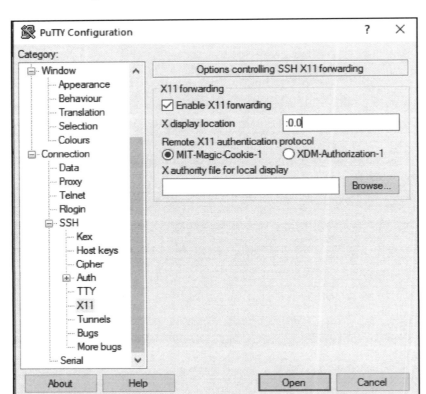

 Do not open the Putty session yet navigate back to the session window.

4. Right-click on the VM and navigate to **Settings | Network**. Enable the network **Adapter 2** ensure the settings are configured as **Attached to: Host-only Adapter** and **Name: VirtualBox Host-Only Ethernet Adapter.**

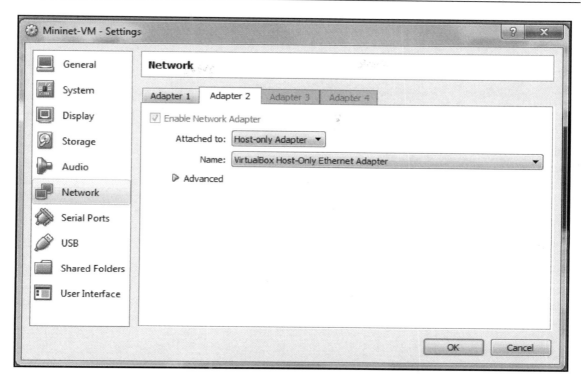

3. Start the Mininet VM image in the virtualization program of your choice (VirtualBox is shown in the following screenshot):

4. Log in to the Mininet VM using the default username and password. The default username and password are both `mininet`. The root account is not enabled for login and you can use `sudo` to execute a command with superuser privileges.

5. In order to establish an SSH session to the Mininet VM, you have to find the IP address of the VM. This address for VirtualBox is probably in the range of 192.168.x.y. Type the following command in the VM console:

```
/sbin/ifconfig eth0
```

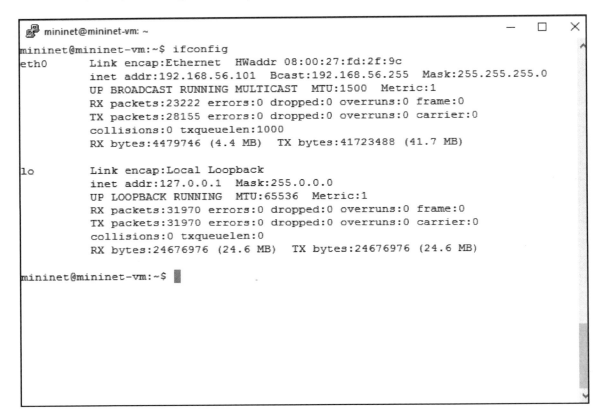

```
mininet@mininet-vm: ~                                    —   □    ×
mininet@mininet-vm:~$ ifconfig
eth0      Link encap:Ethernet  HWaddr 08:00:27:fd:2f:9c
          inet addr:192.168.56.101  Bcast:192.168.56.255  Mask:255.255.255.0
          UP BROADCAST RUNNING MULTICAST  MTU:1500  Metric:1
          RX packets:23222 errors:0 dropped:0 overruns:0 frame:0
          TX packets:28155 errors:0 dropped:0 overruns:0 carrier:0
          collisions:0 txqueuelen:1000
          RX bytes:4479746 (4.4 MB)  TX bytes:41723488 (41.7 MB)

lo        Link encap:Local Loopback
          inet addr:127.0.0.1  Mask:255.0.0.0
          UP LOOPBACK RUNNING  MTU:65536  Metric:1
          RX packets:31970 errors:0 dropped:0 overruns:0 frame:0
          TX packets:31970 errors:0 dropped:0 overruns:0 carrier:0
          collisions:0 txqueuelen:0
          RX bytes:24676976 (24.6 MB)  TX bytes:24676976 (24.6 MB)

mininet@mininet-vm:~$ 
```

6. You can SSH to the VM using the putty window open previously as follows. Also, the Putty session configuration can be saved for future logins:

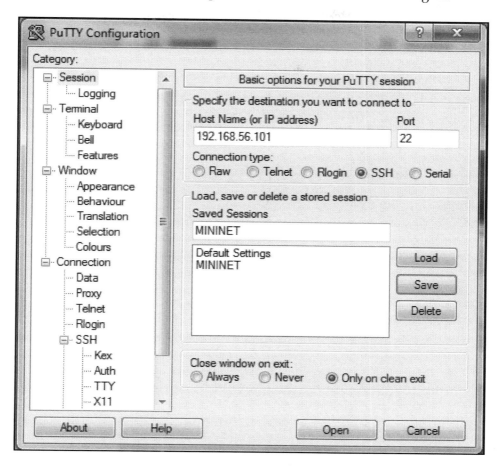

7. In the following screenshot, you can see the experimental environment based on VMware Player, Mininet, Xming (X-Server), and Putty (SSH terminal). You can see that we have logged in to the Mininet VM using PuTTY (SSH client) and then we have started the Wireshark as a background process (that is, `sudo wireshark &`). Since the X11 forwarding is enabled, the Wireshark GUI appears as a separate window:

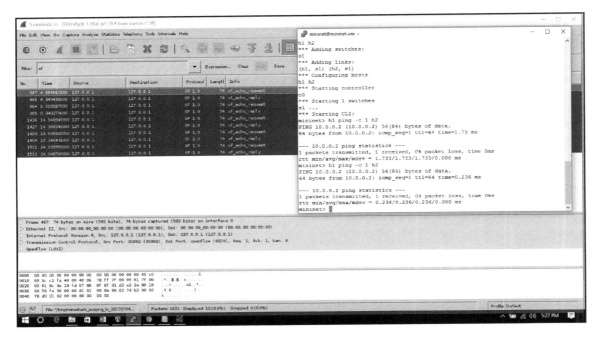

OpenFlow laboratory using Mininet

8. Before starting the Mininet emulator, you have to select the **Capture** device in Wireshark (lo or loopback interface) and start capturing the traffic. In order to display the OpenFlow related traffic, you have to add (OpenFlow) in the filter box of Wireshark and apply it to the capturing traffic. This will instruct Wireshark to just display OpenFlow related traffic. Since Mininet has not been started yet, no OpenFlow packets should be displayed in the main window of Wireshark. In the next section, you will run a sample experiment using Mininet.

The Mininet VM does not include a desktop manager. The graphic output should be forwarded via X forwarding through SSH. You can consult the following FAQ to enable X11 forwarding. Setting X11 up correctly will enable you to run other GUI programs and the xterm terminal emulator used later in this chapter. For more information, visit `https://github.com/mininet/mininet/wiki/FAQ#x11-forwarding`.

Experimenting with Mininet

Mininet enables you to quickly create, customize, interact with, and share an OpenFlow prototype. Mininet's command line can be used to create a network (hosts and switches). Its CLI allows you to control and manage your entire virtual network from a single console. Furthermore, Mininet's API allows you to develop custom network applications with a few lines of Python script. Once a prototype works on Mininet, it can be deployed on a real network.

In this sample experiment, we will use the default topology of Mininet (by running `$ sudo mn`). This topology includes one OpenFlow switch connected to two hosts, plus the OpenFlow reference controller. This topology can also be specified on the command line with `--topo=minimal`. Other topologies are also available out of the box in Mininet; refer to the `--topo` section in the output of `mn -h`. You can display nodes, links, and dump information about all nodes in the setup using the following commands, respectively:

```
$ sudo mn
mininet> nodes
result:
available nodes are:
c0 h1 h2 s1
mininet> net
result:
h1 h1-eth0:s1-eth1
h2 h2-eth0:s1-eth2
s1 lo:  s1-eth1:h1-eth0 s1-eth2:h2-eth0
c0
mininet> dump
result:
<Host h1: h1-eth0:10.0.0.1 pid=5066>
<Host h2: h2-eth0:10.0.0.2 pid=5068>
<OVSSwitch s1: lo:127.0.0.1,s1-eth1:None,s1-eth2:None pid=5073>
<Controller c0: 127.0.0.1:6653 pid=5059>
```

Upon execution of the Mininet emulation environment with the default topology, the OpenFlow controller and switch initiate the OpenFlow protocol, which can be captured and viewed in the Wireshark capturing window. The following screenshot shows the captured traffic, which shows the Hello message, feature request/reply and several packet-in messages. This confirms that the OpenFlow switch in this setup is connected to the OpenFlow controller:

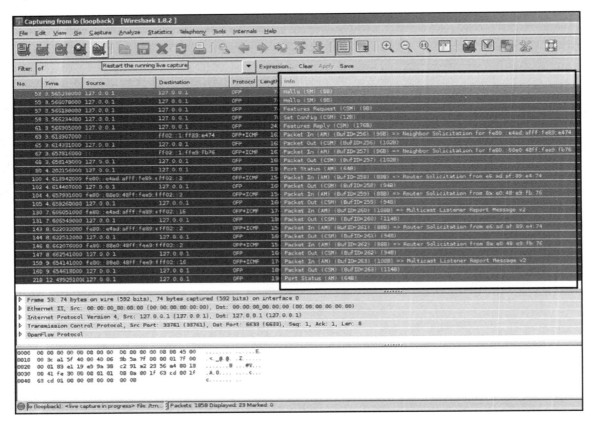

OpenFlow traffic, which is captured in Wireshark

If the first string typed into the Mininet CLI (mininet>) is a host, switch, or controller name, the command is executed on that node. For example, you can see the Ethernet and loopback interface of the first host (h1) using the following command:

```
mininet> h1 ifconfig -a
```

Now we can check the connectivity of each host with a simple `ping` command:

```
mininet> h1 ping -c 1 h2
```

This command sends a single ping packet from h1 to h2. The first host (h1) ARP for the MAC address of the second (h2) causes a `packet_in` message to go to the OpenFlow controller. The controller then sends a `packet_out` message to flood the broadcast packet to other ports on the switch (in this example, the only other data port). The second host observes the ARP request and sends a broadcast reply. This reply goes to the controller, which sends it to the first host and pushes down a flow entry to the flow table of s1 (OpenFlow switch):

The captured traffic after issuing an h1 ping -c 1 h2 command in Mininet

Now the first host knows the IP address of the second and can send its ping via an **Internet Control Message Protocol (ICMP)** echo request. This request and its corresponding reply from the second host both go to the controller and result in a flow entry pushed down. The actual packets are sent out too. In our setup, the reported ping time is 3.93 ms. We repeat the same `ping` command one more time:

```
mininet> h1 ping -c 1 h2
```

The ping time for the second `ping` command is decreased to just 0.25 ms. A flow entry covering ICMP ping traffic was previously installed in the switch, so no control traffic was generated and the packets immediately pass through the switch.

An easier way to run this test is to use the Mininet CLI built-in `pingall` command, which does an all-pairs ping. Another useful test is a self-contained regression test. The following command created a minimal topology, started up the OpenFlow reference controller, ran an all-pairs-ping test, and tore down both the topology and the controller:

```
$ sudo mn --test pingpair
```

Another useful test is the performance evaluation using `iperf`:

```
$ sudo mn --test iperf
```

This command needs a few seconds to complete. It creates the same Mininet topology (one controller, one switch, and two hosts) and runs an `iperf` server on one host, an `iperf` client on the second host, and reports the TCP bandwidth between these two hosts.

Using Mininet's Python API, it is possible to define custom topologies for experiments. A built-in example is provided in `~/mininet/custom/topo-2sw-2host.py`. This example connects two switches directly, with a single host connected to each switch:

```
"""Custom topology example
Two directly connected switches plus a host for each switch:
   host --- switch --- switch --- host
  h1 <-> s3 <-> s4 <-> h2
Adding the 'topos' dict with a key/value pair to generate our newly defined
topology enables one to pass in '--topo=mytopo' from the command line.
"""
from mininet.topo import Topo
class MyTopo( Topo ):
    "Simple topology example."
    def __init__( self ):
        "Create custom topo."
        # Initialize topology
        Topo.__init__( self )
        # Add hosts and switches
        leftHost = self.addHost( 'h1' )
        rightHost = self.addHost( 'h2' )
        leftSwitch = self.addSwitch( 's3' )
        rightSwitch = self.addSwitch( 's4' )
        # Add links
        self.addLink( leftHost, leftSwitch )
        self.addLink( leftSwitch, rightSwitch )
        self.addLink( rightSwitch, rightHost )
        topos = { 'mytopo': ( lambda: MyTopo() ) }
```

This Python script can be passed as a command-line parameter to the Mininet. When a custom Mininet file is provided, it can add new topologies, switch types, and tests to the command line. For instance, a `pingall` test can be executed using the mentioned topology with the following invocation of Mininet:

```
$ sudo mn --custom ~/mininet/custom/topo-2sw-2host.py --topo mytopo
--test pingall
```

For more complex debugging and to have access to the console of hosts, switch(es), or controller(s), you can start Mininet with the `-x` command-line parameter (that is, `sudo mn -x`). The xterms, which will pop up, are useful for running interactive commands. For instance, in the xterm labeled, switch: s1 (root), you can run this:

```
# dpctl dump-flows tcp:127.0.0.1:6634
```

Since the flow table of the switch s1 is empty, nothing will print out. Now in the xterm of host 1 (h1), you can ping the other host (h2) using a normal `ping` command (`# ping 10.0.0.2`). If you go back to the xterm of switch s1 and dump the flow table, you should see multiple flow entries now. You can also use the `dpctl` built-in command in Mininet.

This was just a brief introduction to Mininet. In next chapters, we will use Mininet as part of our setup for experimenting with OpenFlow controllers and for the development of network applications. Those of you interested can find more details on the Mininet website at `http://mininet.org/`.

Experimenting with Mininet GUI (MiniEdit)

Mininet network simulator comes with a Python-based application that provides a simple GUI editor for Mininet. This tool was developed to further expatiate on the extension of Mininet. Using MiniEdit for network building, network elements configuration, configuration setup, and running simulated networks will be covered in the next session.

Getting started with MiniEdit

MiniEdit comes with a very simple interface canvas with icons that represent various tools. To open the interface, you have to run the following, which is the interface presented by MiniEdit that includes various tool icons:

```
$ sudo ~/mininet/examples/miniedit.py
```

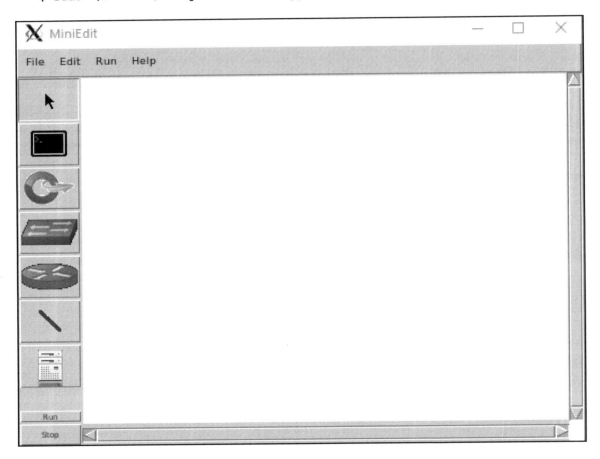

- **Select tool**: This is typically used for the movement of nodes on the canvas
- **Host tool**: This is used to create end-host nodes on the canvas
- **Switch tool**: This is used to create an OpenFlow-enabled switch on the canvas
- **Legacy Switch tool**: This is used to create a traditional learning Ethernet switch with default settings on the canvas
- **Legacy Router tool**: This is used to create an independently functioning legacy router used for IP forwarding on the canvas
- **NetLink tool**: This is used to create links between the nodes on the canvas
- **Controller tool**: This is used to create an OpenFlow-supported controller
- **Run** and **Stop** tool: These are used to start and stop the Mininet simulation that is currently presented on the MiniEdit canvas

Creating a custom topology on Mininet canvas

In order to create a complete custom topology on the Mininet canvas, you will be required to use the tools that were introduced in the section:

1. First, we will begin with placing the hosts on the canvas. To achieve this, you have to click on the host tool and then go to the canvas and click on the point you need the host to appear on. After doing that, the host will be created and it will be done in a sequential order, that is, **h1**, **h2**, **h3**, and so on.

2. Next, we have to place the desired switch on the canvas. In this demonstration, we are using the OpenFlow enabled switch. Click on the switch tool and place it just like the host was placed earlier.

3. The controllers should also be placed as it was done for the hosts and switches.

4. We then have to connect the devices with links between them. Clicking on the NetLink tool, you click on the first device you wish to connect and then click on the other device.

5. In the MiniEdit canvas, a host should be connected to a switch, every switch to another switch, then one of the switches must be connected to the controller.

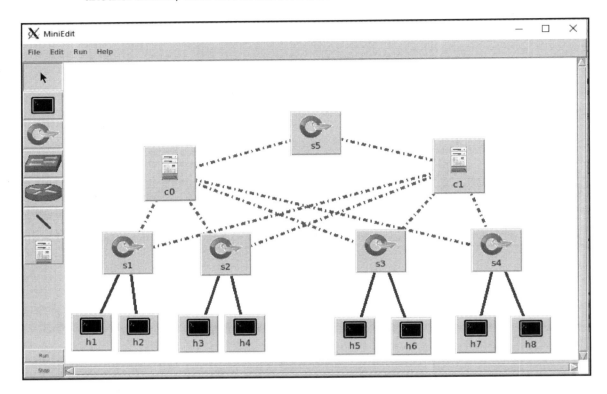

Configuring the controller

The topology that was created on the MiniEdit canvas constitutes of two default OpenFlow controllers. Every controller that is placed on the canvas is created with the default settings that are shown in the following screenshot. To create a stable topology, it is required that each controller operate on a unique port. By default, the controllers port are created with the same port number 6633. You are required to change the port number of every other controller; in this setup, we have controller c0 take port 6633 and controller c1 take port 6634:

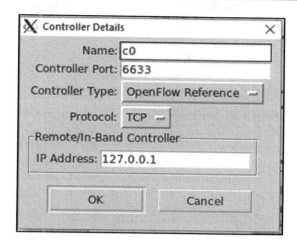

Configuring the switch

The switches in the MiniEdit environment can have their operational parameters edited; these parameters include the hostname, IP addresses, interfaces, and so on. This is an screenshot of the parameters that can be edited on the switch:

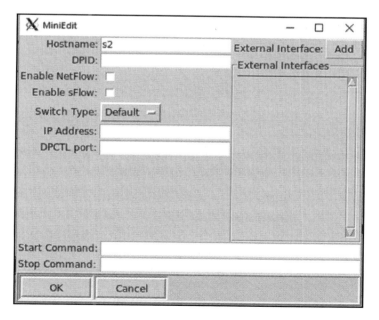

Configuring the host

The hosts that exist in the MiniEdit canvas can have their parameters edited as well. These parameters include the hostname, IP address, CPU allocation, and interface configurations. The following screenshot shows the parameters that could be set in the host setting:

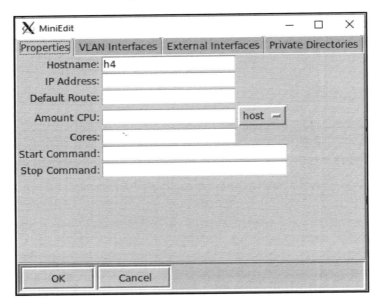

Setting the MiniEdit preferences

It is required that the MiniEdit preferences are always set before the network topology is started. To access it, go to the **Edit** tab and then click on **Preferences**. In the **Preference** tab, we have the option of selecting various parameters for the simulation. Attention should be paid to **IP Base**, **Default Switch**, and the OpenFlow version that should be used.

In our demonstration, we will be using **OpenFlow 1.0** and enabling the **Start CLI** option so we can access the Mininet CLI:

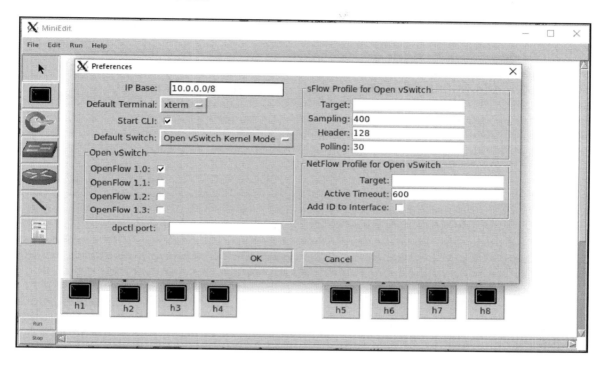

Saving the configuration

On creating the topology in the MiniEdit canvas and running same topology, we have to save the configuration. Saved configuration can be in two formats:

- **Mininet topology**: Files saved in this format are saved in the *.mn format. To save the file in this format, click on **File** at the top and select **Save** in the menu dropped down. Type the filename and save the file.
- **Custom Mininet script**: Files saved in this format are saved in the *.py format. These files can be run as a Python file because of the file extension. To save the file in this format, click on the **File** at the top and select **Save Level 2 Script**. Type the file name and save the file.

The files saved are stored in any directory of the VM and can be loaded any time. You can see the following screenshot while saving the Mininet topology:

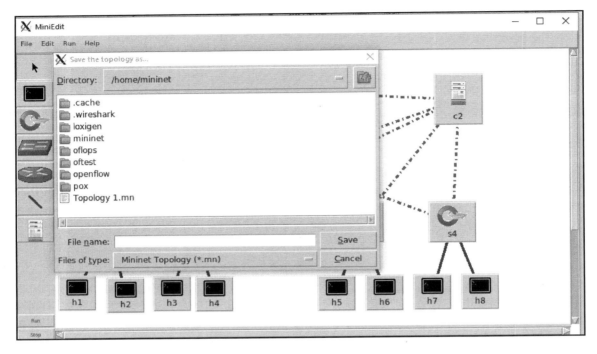

Mininet Topology

While saving the custom Mininet topology you can see the following screenshot:

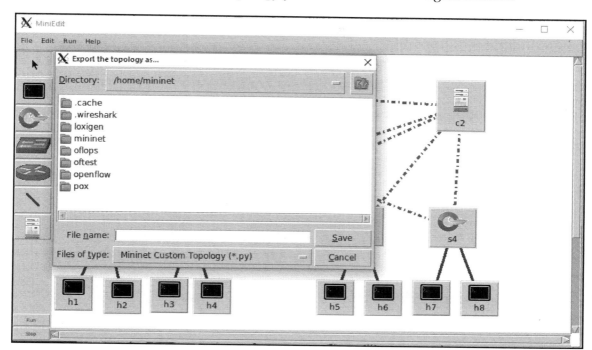

Custom Mininet Script

Running a Mininet topology simulation, generating logs, and monitoring the flow table

In order to further explain how MiniEdit runs a simulation, we will run the simulation of the given preceding topology. In this simulation, we will monitor the flow of traffic using Wireshark; the flow table will also be monitored on the OpenFlow enables switch, and to achieve this, we shall be pinging from host 1 to host 2. The steps taken are listed as follows and the figure shows the captured result:

1. Click on **Run** at the bottom of the page to start the simulation process.
2. Right-click on the host 1 (**h1**), open the terminal and type the `sudo wireshark & command to open the Wireshark packet monitor.
3. In the Wireshark filter pane, input `of` to filter just the OpenFlow protocol

4. Set the capture interface as `eth1` of the h1 device.

5. In the terminal of the host 1, type `Ping 10.0.0.2` in order to ping host 2.

6. The Wireshark then captures the traffic traversing the interface.

7. In order to check the flow tables on the switch 1, you have to run the `sudo ovs-ofctl dump flow s1` command.

The following screenshot shows the result of pings from host 1 to host 2, monitoring the Wireshark interface and the flow tables present in switch 1:

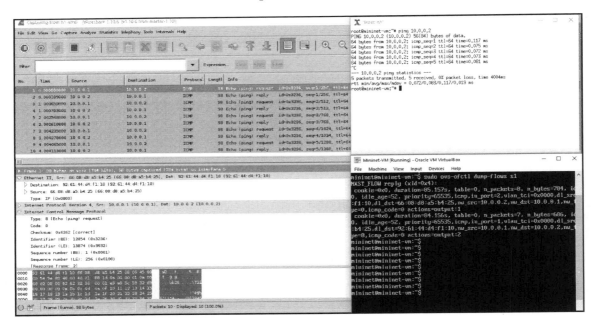

Summary

The reference implementation of OpenFlow switch includes `ofdatapath`, which implements the flow table in user space; `ofprotocol`, a program that implements the secure channel component of the reference switch; and `dpctl`, which is a tool for configuring the switch. There are three main message types in OpenFlow protocol (controller-to-switch, asynchronous, and symmetric messages). In addition to hardware OpenFlow switches, there is a software implementation of OpenFlow in the from of soft-switches. Mininet is a network emulator that runs a collection of end hosts, switches, and links on a single Linux kernel.

In this chapter, we presented and used Mininet as an OpenFlow laboratory on a single computer and introduced MiniEdit, a vital tool in a Mininet simulation. In the next chapter, we will cover different SDN/OpenFlow controller options.

4

The OpenFlow Controllers

This chapter covers the role of the OpenFlow controllers, the interface to the switch, and the provided API for **network applications** (**Net Apps**). We will also see:

- The overall functionality of the OpenFlow (SDN) controllers
- The existing implementations (including NOX/POX, NodeFlow, Floodlight, **OpenDaylight** (**ODL**), and Ryu)
- Special controllers or applications over controllers (FlowVisor and RouteFlow)

Software-Defined Networking controllers

The decoupled control and data plane architecture of **Software-Defined Networking** (**SDN**), as depicted in the following diagram, and in particular OpenFlow can be compared with an operating system and computer hardware. The OpenFlow controller (similar to the operating system) provides a programmatic interface to the OpenFlow switches (similar to computer hardware). Using this programmatic interface, network applications, referred to as Net Apps, can be written to perform control and management tasks and offer new functionalities. The control plane in SDN and OpenFlow in particular is logically centralized, and Net Apps are written as if the network is a single system.

With a reactive control model, the OpenFlow switches must consult an OpenFlow controller each time a decision must be made, such as when a new packet flow reaches an OpenFlow switch (that is, `packet_in` event). In the case of flow-based control granularity, there will be a small performance delay as the first packet of each new flow is forwarded to the controller for a decision (for example, forward or drop), after which future traffic within that flow will be forwarded at line rate within the switching hardware. While the first-packet delay is negligible in many cases, it may be a concern if the central OpenFlow controller is geographically remote or if most flows are short-lived (for example, as single-packet flows). An alternative proactive approach is also possible in OpenFlow to push policy rules out from the controller to the switches.

While this simplifies the control, management, and policy enforcement tasks, the bindings must be closely maintained between the controller and OpenFlow switches. The first important concern of this centralized control is the scalability of the system and the second one is the placement of controllers. A recent study of the several OpenFlow controller implementations (NOX-MT, Maestro, and Beacon), conducted on a large emulated network with 100,000 hosts and up to 256 switches, revealed that all OpenFlow controllers were able to handle at least 50,000 new flow requests per second in each of the experimental scenarios. Furthermore, new OpenFlow controllers under development, such as Mc-Nettle (http://haskell.cs.yale.edu/other-projects/nettle/mcnettle/) target powerful multi-core servers and are being designed to scale up to large data center workloads (for example, 20 million flow requests per second and up to 5,000 switches).

In packet switching networks, traditionally, each packet contains the required information for a network switch to make individual routing decisions. However, most applications send data as a flow of many individual packets. The control granularity in OpenFlow is in the scale of flows, not packets. When controlling individual flows, the decision made for the first packet of the flow can be applied to all the subsequent packets of the flow within the data plane (OpenFlow switches).

The overhead may be further reduced by grouping the flows together, such as all traffic between two hosts, and performing control decisions on the aggregated flows.

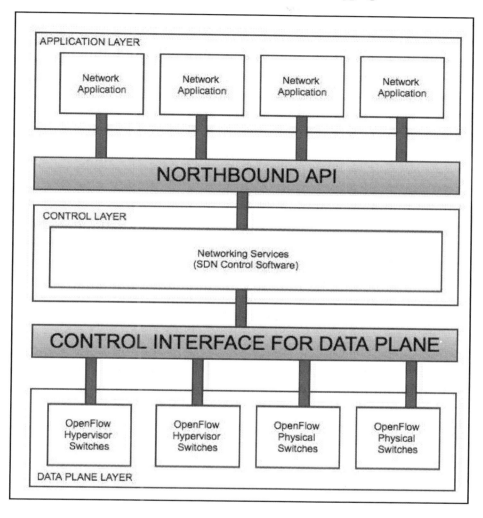

The role of the controller in the SDN approach

Multiple controllers may be used to reduce the latency or increase the scalability and fault tolerance of the OpenFlow (SDN) deployment. OpenFlow allows the connection of multiple controllers to a switch, which would allow backup controllers to take over in the event of a failure. Onix, HyperFlow, ONOS, DISCO, and Elastic{ON} take the idea further by attempting to maintain a logically centralized, but physically distributed control plane. This decreases the lookup overhead by enabling communication with local controllers, while still allowing applications to be written with a simplified central view of the network. The potential main downside of this approach is maintaining the consistent state in the overall distributed system. This may cause Net Apps that believe they have an accurate view of the network to act incorrectly due to inconsistency in the global network state.

Recalling the operating system analogy, an OpenFlow controller acts as a network operating system and should implement at least two interfaces: a **southbound** interface that allows OpenFlow switches to communicate with the controller, and a **northbound** interface that presents a programmable **Application Programming Interface (API)** to network control and management applications (that is, Net Apps). External control and management systems/software or network services may wish to extract information about the underlying network or enforce policies, or control an aspect of the network behavior. Besides, a primary OpenFlow controller may need to share policy information with a backup controller, or communicate with other controllers across multiple control domains. While the southbound interface (for example, OpenFlow or ForCES: `https://datatracker.ietf.org/wg/forces/charter/`) is well defined and can be considered as a de facto standard, there is no widely accepted standard for northbound interactions, and they are more likely to be implemented on a use-case basis for particular applications.

Existing implementations

Currently, there are different OpenFlow (and SDN) controller implementations, which we will introduce in more detail in `Chapter 9`, *Open Source Resources*, as part of existing open source projects. In this chapter, we limit ourselves to NOX, POX, NodeFlow, Floodlight (which is forked from Beacon), ODL, and Ryu to present some OpenFlow controllers and different possibilities for choosing a programming language to develop the network applications.

NOX and POX

NOX (https://github.com/noxrepo/) was the first OpenFlow controller written in C++ and it provides an API for Python too. It has been the basis for many research and development projects in the early exploration of the OpenFlow and SDN space. NOX has two separate lines of development:

- NOX-Classic
- NOX, also known as new NOX

The former is the well-known line of development, which contains support for Python and C++ along with a bunch of network applications. However, this line of development is deprecated and there is no plan for further development on NOX-Classic. New NOX only supports C++. It has fewer network applications compared to NOX-Classic, but is much faster and has a much cleaner code base.

POX is a Python-only version of NOX. It can be considered as a general, open source OpenFlow controller written in Python, and a platform for rapid development and prototyping of network applications. The primary target of POX is research. Since many research projects are short-lived by nature, the focus of the developers of POX is on the right interfaces rather than maintaining a stable API.

NOX (and POX) are managed in Git source code repositories on GitHub. Cloning the Git repository is the preferred way to get NOX and POX. POX branches fall into two categories: active and released. Active branches are branches that are being actively developed. Released branches are branches which at some point were selected as being a new version. The most recently released branch may continue to get worked on, but only in the form of bug fixes; new features always go into the active branch. You can get the latest version of NOX and POX with the following commands:

```
$ git clone https://github.com/noxrepo/nox
$ git clone http://www.github.com/noxrepo/pox
```

In Chapter 3, *Implementing the OpenFlow Switch*, we set up the OpenFlow laboratory using the Mininet emulation environment. In this section, we start with a Net App, which behaves as a simple Ethernet hub. You can change it to a learning Ethernet L2 switch as an exercise. In this application, the switch will examine each packet and learn the source-port mapping. Thereafter, the source MAC address will be associated with the port.

If the destination of the packet is already associated with some port, the packet will be sent to the given port, or else it will be flooded on all ports of the switch. The first step is to start your OpenFlow VM. Then you need to download POX into your VM:

```
$ git clone http://github.com/noxrepo/pox
$ cd pox
```

Running a POX application

After getting the POX controller, you can try running a basic hub example in POX as follows:

```
$ cd pox
$ ./pox.py log.level --DEBUG misc.of_tutorial
```

This command line tells POX to enable verbose logging and to start the of_tutorial component, which you will be using. This of_tutorial component acts as an Ethernet hub. Now you can start the Mininet OpenFlow laboratory using the following command line:

```
$ sudo mn --topo single,3 --mac --switch ovsk --controller remote
```

The switches may take a little bit of time to connect. When an OpenFlow switch loses its connection to a controller, it will generally increase the period between which it attempts to contact the controller, up to a maximum of 15 seconds. This timer is implementation specific and can be defined by the user. Since the OpenFlow switch has not connected yet, this delay may be anything between 0 and 15 seconds. If this is too long to wait, the switch can be configured to wait no more than N seconds using the --max-backoff parameter. Wait until the application indicates that the OpenFlow switch has connected. When the switch connects, POX will print something like the following:

```
INFO:openflow.of_01:[Con 1/1] Connected to 00-00-00-00-00-01
DEBUG:samples.of_tutorial:Controlling [Con 1/1]
```

The first line is the portion of POX that handles OpenFlow connections. The second line is the tutorial component itself.

Now, we verify that the hosts can ping each other and that all the hosts see the exact same traffic: the behavior of a hub. To do this, we will create xterms for each host and view the traffic in each. In the Mininet console, start up three xterms:

```
mininet> xterm h1 h2 h3
```

Arrange each xterm so that they're all on the screen at once. This may require reducing the height to fit on a cramped laptop screen. In the xterms for h2 and h3, run tcpdump, a utility to print the packets seen by a host:

```
# tcpdump -XX -n -i h2-eth0
# tcpdump -XX -n -i h3-eth0
```

In the xterm for h1, issue a ping command:

```
# ping -c1 10.0.0.2
```

The ping packets are now going up to the controller, which then floods them out of all interfaces except the sending one. You should see identical ARP and ICMP packets corresponding to the ping in both xterms running tcpdump. This is how a hub works: it sends all packets to every port on the network. Now, see what happens when a non-existent host doesn't reply. From the h1 xterm:

```
# ping -c1 10.0.0.5
```

You should see three unanswered ARP requests in the tcpdump xterms. If your code is off later, three unanswered ARP requests is a signal that you might be accidentally dropping packets. You can close the xterms now.

In order to change the behavior of the hub to a learning switch, you have to add the learning switch functionality to of_tutorial.py. Go to your SSH terminal and stop the tutorial hub controller by pressing *Ctrl + C*. The file you'll modify is pox/misc/of_tutorial.py. Open pox/misc/of_tutorial.py in your favorite editor. The current code calls act_like_hub() from the handler for packet_in messages to implement the switch behavior. You will want to switch to using the act_like_switch() function, which contains a sketch of what your final learning switch code should look like. Each time you change and save this file, make sure to restart POX, then use pings to verify the behavior of the combination of switch and controller as the following:

- Hub
- Controller-based Ethernet learning switch
- Flow-accelerated learning switch

For the second and third use cases, hosts that are not the destination for a ping should display no `tcpdump` traffic after the initial broadcast ARP request. Python is a dynamic and interpreted language. There is no separate compilation step; just update your code and rerun it. Python has built-in hash tables, called dictionaries, and vectors, called lists. Some of the common operations that you need for a learning switch are as follows:

- To initialize a dictionary:

```
mactable = {}
```

- To add an element to a dictionary:

```
mactable[0x123] = 2
```

- To check for dictionary membership:

```
if 0x123 in mactable:
    print 'element 2 is in mactable'
if 0x123 not in mactable:
    print 'element 2 is not in mactable'
```

- To print a debug message in POX:

```
log.debug('saw new MAC!')
```

- To print an error message in POX:

```
log.error('unexpected packet causing system meltdown!')
```

- To print all member variables and functions of an object:

```
print dir(object)
```

- To comment a line of code:

```
# Prepend comments with a #; no // or /**/
```

You can find more Python resources at the following URLs:

- List of built-in functions in Python: `https://docs.python.org/2/library/functions.html`
- Official Python tutorial: `https://docs.python.org/2/tutorial/`

In addition to the preceding functions, you also need some details about the POX APIs, which are useful for the development of learning switch. There is also other documentation available in the appropriate section of POX's website.

Sending OpenFlow messages with POX:

```
connection.send( ... ) # send an OpenFlow message to a switch
```

When a connection to a switch starts, a `ConnectionUp` event is fired. The example code creates a new `Tutorial` object that holds a reference to the associated `Connection` object. This can later be used to send commands (OpenFlow messages) to the switch:

```
ofp_action_output class
```

This is an action for use with `ofp_packet_out` and `ofp_flow_mod`. It specifies a switch port that you wish to send the packet out of. It can also take various special port numbers. An example of this would be `OFPP_FLOOD`, which sends the packet out on all ports except the one the packet originally arrived on. The following example creates an output action that would send packets to all ports:

```
out_action = of.ofp_action_output(port = of.OFPP_FLOOD)
ofp_match class
```

Objects of this class describe packet header fields and an input port to match on. All fields are optional; items that are not specified are wildcards, and will match on anything. Some notable fields of `ofp_match` objects are:

- `dl_src`: The data link layer (MAC) source address
- `dl_dst`: The data link layer (MAC) destination address
- `in_port`: The packet input switch port

For example: Create a match that matches packets arriving on port 3:

```
match = of.ofp_match()
match.in_port = 3
ofp_packet_out OpenFlow message
```

The `ofp_packet_out` message instructs a switch to send a packet. The packet might be constructed at the controller, or it might be the one that the switch received, buffered, and forwarded to the controller (and is now referenced by a `buffer_id`). Notable fields are:

- `buffer_id`: The `buffer_id` of a buffer you wish to send. Do not set if you are sending a constructed packet.
- `data`: Raw bytes you wish the switch to send. Do not set if you are sending a buffered packet.
- `actions`: A list of actions to apply (for this tutorial, this is just a single `ofp_action_output action`).
- `in_port`: The port number this packet initially arrived on if you are sending by `buffer_id`, otherwise `OFPP_NONE`.

For example: The `send_packet()` method `of_tutorial`:

```python
def send_packet (self, buffer_id, raw_data, out_port, in_port):
  """
  Sends a packet out of the specified switch port.
  If buffer_id is a valid buffer on the switch, use that.
   Otherwise, send the raw data in raw_data.
  The "in_port" is the port number that packet arrived on.  Use
  OFPP_NONE if you're generating this packet.
  """
  msg = of.ofp_packet_out ()
  msg.in_port = in_port
  if buffer_id != -1 and buffer_id is not None:
    # We got a buffer ID from the switch; use that
    msg.buffer_id = buffer_id
  else:
    # No buffer ID from switch -- we got the raw data
    if raw_data is None:
      # No raw_data specified -- nothing to send!
      return
    msg.data = raw_data
  action = of.ofp_action_output (port = out_port)
  msg.actions.append (action)
  # Send message to switch
  self.connection.send (msg)
ofp_flow_mod OpenFlow message
```

This instructs a switch to install a flow table entry. Flow table entries match some fields of the incoming packets and execute some list of actions on the matching packets. The actions are the same as for `ofp_packet_out`, mentioned previously (and again, for the tutorial, all you need is the simple `ofp_action_output` action). The match is described by an `ofp_match` object. Notable fields are:

- `idle_timeout`: Number of idle seconds before the flow entry is removed. Defaults to no idle timeout.
- `hard_timeout`: Number of seconds before the flow entry is removed. Defaults to no timeout.
- `actions`: A list of actions to be performed on matching packets (for example, `ofp_action_output`).
- `priority`: When using non-exact (wildcarded) matches, this specifies the priority for overlapping matches. Higher values have higher priority. Not important for exact or non-overlapping entries.
- `buffer_id`: The `buffer_id` field of a buffer to apply the actions to immediately. Leave unspecified for none.
- `in_port`: If using a `buffer_id`, this is the associated input port.
- `match`: An `ofp_match` object. By default, this matches everything, so you should probably set some of its fields.

For example: Create a `flow_mod` that sends packets from port 3 out of port 4:

```
fm = of.ofp_flow_mod()
fm.match.in_port = 3
fm.actions.append(of.ofp_action_output(port = 4))
```

 For more information about OpenFlow constants, see the main OpenFlow types/enums/`structs` file, `openflow.h`, in `~/openflow/include/openflow/openflow.h`. You may also wish to consult POX's OpenFlow library in `pox/openflow/libopenflow_01.py` and, of course, the OpenFlow 1.0 specification.

The POX packet library is used to parse packets and make each protocol field available to Python. This library can also be used to construct packets for sending. The parsing libraries are present in `pox/lib/packet/`.

Each protocol has a corresponding parsing file. For the first exercise, you'll only need to access the Ethernet source and destination fields. To extract the source of a packet, use the dot notation:

```
packet.src
```

The Ethernet `src` and `dst` fields are stored as `pox.lib.addresses.EthAddr` objects. These can easily be converted to their common string representation (`str(addr)` will return something like `"01:ea:be:02:05:01"`), or be created from their common string representation (`EthAddr("01:ea:be:02:05:01")`). To see all members of a parsed packet object:

```
print dir(packet)
```

Here's what you'd see for an ARP packet:

```
['HW_TYPE_ETHERNET', 'MIN_LEN', 'PROTO_TYPE_IP', 'REPLY', 'REQUEST',
'REV_REPLY',
 'REV_REQUEST', '__class__', '__delattr__', '__dict__', '__doc__',
'__format__',
 '__getattribute__', '__hash__', '__init__', '__len__', '__module__',
'__new__',
 '__nonzero__', '__reduce__', '__reduce_ex__', '__repr__', '__setattr__',
 '__sizeof__', '__str__', '__subclasshook__', '__weakref__', '_init',
'err',
 'find', 'hdr', 'hwdst', 'hwlen', 'hwsrc', 'hwtype', 'msg', 'next',
'opcode',
 'pack', 'parse', 'parsed', 'payload', 'pre_hdr', 'prev', 'protodst',
'protolen',
 'protosrc', 'prototype', 'raw', 'set_payload', 'unpack', 'warn']
```

Many fields are common to all the Python objects and can be ignored, but this can be a quick way to avoid a trip to a function's documentation.

NodeFlow

NodeFlow (http://garyberger.net/?p=537, developed by Gary Berger, technical leader, office of the CTO of Cisco Systems) is a minimalist OpenFlow controller written in JavaScript for Node.js (https://nodejs.org/en/). Node.js is a server-side software system designed for writing scalable internet applications (for example, HTTP servers). It can be considered as a packaged compilation of Google's V8 JavaScript engine, the libuv platform abstraction layer, and a core library, which is written in JavaScript. Node.js uses an event-driven, non-blocking I/O model that makes it lightweight and efficient, perfect for data-intensive real-time applications that run across distributed devices. Programs are written on the server side in JavaScript, using event-driven, asynchronous I/O to minimize overhead and maximize the scalability. Therefore, unlike most JavaScript programs, the program is not executed in a web browser. Instead, it runs as a server-side JavaScript application. NodeFlow is actually a very simple program and relies heavily on a protocol interpreter called **OFLIB-NODE** written by Zoltan LaJos Kis.

NodeFlow is an experimental system available on GitHub (https://github.com/gaberger/NodeFLow) along with a fork of the OFLIB-NODE libraries (https://github.com/gaberger/oflib-node). The beauty of NodeFlow is its simplicity in running and understanding an OpenFlow controller with fewer than 500 lines of code. Leveraging JavaScript and the high-performance Google V8 JavaScript engine enables network architects to experiment with various SDN features without the need to deal with all of the boilerplate code required for setting up event-driven programming.

The NodeFlow server (that is, OpenFlow controller) instantiates with a simple call to net.createServer. The address and listening port are configured through a start script:

```
NodeFlowServer.prototype.start = function(address, port) {
var self = this
var socket = []
var server = net.createServer()
server.listen(port, address, function(err, result) {
util.log("NodeFlow listening on:" + address + '@' + port)
self.emit('started', { "Config": server.address() })
})
})
```

The next step is to create a unique session ID, from which the controller can keep track of each of the different switch connections. The event listener maintains the socket. The main event-processing loop is invoked whenever data is received from the socket channel. The stream library is utilized to buffer the data and return the decoded OpenFlow message in a `msgs` object. The `msg` object is passed to the `_processMessage` function for further processing:

```
server.on('connection',
  function(socket) {
    socket.setNoDelay(noDelay = true)
    var sessionID = socket.remoteAddress + ":" + socket.remotePort
    sessions[sessionID] = new sessionKeeper(socket)
    util.log("Connection from : " + sessionID)
    socket.on('data', function(data) {
    var msgs = switchStream.process(data);
    msgs.forEach(function(msg) {
    if (msg.hasOwnProperty('message')) {
        self._processMessage(msg, sessionID)
    } else {
        util.log('Error: Cannot parse the message.')
        console.dir(data)
    }
  }
})
```

The last part is the event handlers. `EventEmitters` of Node.js is utilized to trigger the callbacks. These event handlers wait for the specific event to happen and then trigger the processing. NodeFlow handles two specific events: `OFPT_PACKET_IN`, which is the main event to listen to for OpenFlow `PACKET_IN` events, and `SENDPACKET`, which simply encodes and sends out OpenFlow messages:

```
self.on('OFPT_PACKET_IN',
  function(obj) {
  var packet = decode.decodeethernet(obj.message.body.data, 0)
  nfutils.do_l2_learning(obj, packet)
  self._forward_l2_packet(obj, packet)
  })
  self.on('SENDPACKET',
  function(obj) {
  nfutils.sendPacket(obj.type, obj.packet.outmessage,
   obj.packet.sessionID)
  })
```

A simple Net App based on NodeFlow could be a learning switch (following the do_12_learning function). The learning switch simply searches for the source MAC address, and in case the address is not already in the learning table, it will be inserted in the corresponding source port to the forwarding table:

```
do_12_learning: function(obj, packet) {
  self = this
  var dl_src = packet.shost
  var dl_dst = packet.dhost
  var in_port = obj.message.body.in_port
  var dpid = obj.dpid
  if (dl_src == 'ff:ff:ff:ff:ff:ff') {
  return
  }
if (!l2table.hasOwnProperty(dpid)) {
  l2table[dpid] = new Object() //create object
  }
if (l2table[dpid].hasOwnProperty(dl_src)) {
  var dst = l2table[dpid][dl_src]
    if (dst != in_port) {
      util.log("MAC has moved from " + dst + " to " + in_port)
    } else {
        return
    }
} else {
    util.log("learned mac " + dl_src + " port : " + in_port)
    l2table[dpid][dl_src] = in_port
}
  if (debug) {
    console.dir(l2table)
  }
}
```

The complete NodeFlow server is called server.js, which can be downloaded from the NodeFlow Git repository. To run the NodeFlow controller, execute the Node.js code and pass the NodeFlow server (that is, server.js) to the Node.js binary (for example, node.exe on Windows):

```
C:\ program Files\nodejs>node server.js
```

Floodlight

Floodlight is a Java-based OpenFlow controller, based on the Beacon implementation, which supports both physical and virtual OpenFlow switches. Beacon is a cross-platform, modular OpenFlow controller, also implemented in Java. It supports event-based and threaded operation. Beacon was created by David Erickson at Stanford University as a Java-based and cross-platform OpenFlow controller. Prior to being licensed under GPL v2, Floodlight was forked from Beacon, which carries on with an Apache license.

Floodlight has been redesigned without the OSGI framework. Therefore, it can be built, run, and modified without OSGI experience. Besides, Floodlight's community currently includes a number of developers at Big Switch Networks who are actively testing and fixing bugs, and building additional tools, plugins, and features for it. The Floodlight controller is intended to be a platform for a wide variety of Net Apps. Net Apps are important, since they provide solutions to real-world networking problems. One of Floodlight's Net Apps is a circuit pusher.

The circuit pusher creates a flow and provisions switches along the path to the packet's destination. The bidirectional circuit between source and destination is a permanent flow entry on all switches in the route, based on the IP addresses between the two devices with a specific priority.

These are the key characteristics of the circuit pusher:

- The specified end points must be known to the controller before sending a rest API request to the circuit pusher.
- To enable the circuit pusher, you are required to directly execute the `circuitpusher.py` Python code, which is as follows:

```
circuitpusher.py --controller={IP}:{rest port} --type ip
--src {IP} --dst {IP} --add --name {circuit-name}.
```

- The specified end points must be known to the controller before sending a rest API request to the circuit pusher.

Virtual networking filter

This identifies packets that enter the network, but do not match an existing flow. The application determines whether the source and destination are on the same virtual network; if so, the application signals the controller to continue the flow creation. This filter is in fact a simple layer 2 (MAC)-based network virtualization, which enables users to create multiple logical layer 2 networks in a single layer 2 domain.

Important points:

- Enabling the VNK requires starting the Floodlight controller with `quantum.properties` instead of `floodlight.default.properties`.
- Enabling the VNF using curl can be achieved using the following command:

```
curl -X PUT -d '{ "network": { "gateway": "20.0.0.1",
"name": "DemoNetwork" } }'
http://localhost:8080/networkService/v1.1/tenants
/default/networks/DemoNetwork1
```

- For the virtual network:
    - **Name:** DemoNetwork
    - **ID:** DemoNetwork1
    - **Gateway:** 20.0.0.1
    - **Tenant:** default

- Adding a host to the preceding named network DemoNetwork is done using the following command:

```
curl -X PUT -d '{"attachment": {"id": "DemoNetwork",
"mac":"00:00:00:00:00:A2"}}'
http://localhost:8080/networkService/v1.1/tenants/default/
networks/DemoNetwork1/ports/port10/attachment
```

- The host settings are:
    - **MAC address:** 00:00:00:00:00:A2
    - **Port:** port10

Firewall module

Firewall modules give the same protection to devices on SDN as traditional firewalls on a physical network. **Access control list** (**ACL**) rules control whether a flow should be set up to a specific destination. The firewall application has been implemented as a Floodlight module that enforces ACL rules on OpenFlow-enabled switches in the network. The packet monitoring is done using the packet-in messages.

Essential codes used in the firewall module are:

- For enabling the module:

```
curl http://localhost:8080/wm/firewall/module/enable/json -X
PUT -d ''
```

- Adding an allow rule for all flows to pass through switch `00:00:00:00:00:00:00:A5`:

```
curl -X POST -d '{"switchid": "00:00:00:00:00:00:00:A5"}'
http://localhost:8080/wm/firewall/rules/json
```

> The firewall takes an explicit deny rule except when an explicit allow rule is implemented.

- Add an allow rule for UDP to work between IP hosts `20.0.1.14` and `20.0.1.99`, and then block port `25`:

```
curl -X POST -d '{"src-ip": "20.0.1.14 /32", "dst-ip":
"20.0.1.99/32", "dl-type":"ARP" }'
http://localhost:8080/wm/firewall/rules/json
curl -X POST -d '{"dst-ip": "20.0.1.99/32", "dst-ip":
"20.0.1.14 /32", "dl-type":"ARP" }'
http://localhost:8080/wm/firewall/rules/json

curl -X POST -d '{"src-ip": "20.0.1.14 /32", "dst-ip":
"20.0.1.99/32", "nw-proto":"UDP" }'
http://localhost:8080/wm/firewall/rules/json

curl -X POST -d '{"src-ip": "20.0.1.99/32", "dst-ip":
"20.0.1.14 /32", "nw-proto":"UDP" }'
http://localhost:8080/wm/firewall/rules/json

curl -X POST -d '{"src-ip": "20.0.1.14 /32", "dst-ip":
"20.0.1.99/32", "nw-proto":"UDP", "tp-src":"25", "action":"DENY"
```

```
}' http://localhost:8080/wm/firewall/rules/json

curl -X POST -d '{"src-ip": "20.0.1.99/32", "dst-ip":
"20.0.1.14 /32", "nw-proto":"UDP", "tp-src":"25", "action":"DENY"
}' http://localhost:8080/wm/firewall/rules/json
```

Static flow pusher

Floodlight by default operates with reactive entry insertions. The static flow is used to create a flow proactively prior to the initial packet reaching the switches. The static flow pusher is accessible via a REST API and is added by defining the entry in a JSON string, which is then sent to the controller using an HTTP POST by the curl command.

For instance:

```
curl -X POST -d '{"switch":"00:00:00:00:00:00:00:A5", "name":"flow-mod-1",
"cookie":"0", "priority":"32766", "in_port":"1","active":"true",
"actions":"output=2"}'
http://<controller_ip>:8080/wm/staticentrypusher/json
```

Network plugin for OpenStack

Floodlight can be run as a network plugin for OpenStack using Neutron. The Neutron plugin exposes a **Networking-as-a-Service (NaaS)** model via a REST API that is implemented by Floodlight. This solution has two components: a virtual network filter module in Floodlight (that implements the Neutron API) and the Neutron RestProxy plugin that connects Floodlight to Neutron.

Once a Floodlight controller is integrated into OpenStack, network engineers can dynamically provision network resources alongside other virtual and physical computer resources. This improves the overall flexibility and performance.

 For more details and tutorials, see the FloodLight OpenFlowHub page: http://www.projectfloodlight.org/floodlight/.

ODL

ODL is a Linux Foundation Collaborative project (`https://www.opendaylight.org/`), in which a community has come together to fill the need for an open and reference framework for programmability and control through an open source SDN solution. It combines open community developers, open source code, and project governance that guarantees an open, community decision making process on business and technical issues.

ODL can be a core component within any SDN architecture. Building upon an open source SDN controller enables users to reduce operational complexity, extend the lifetime of their existing network infrastructure, and enable new services and capabilities only available with SDN. The mission statement of the ODL project can be read as *OpenDaylight facilitates a community-led, industry-supported open source framework, including code and architecture, to accelerate and advance a common, robust Software-Defined Networking platform.*

ODL is open to anyone. Anyone can develop and contribute code, get elected to the **Technical Steering Committee (TSC)**, get voted onto the board, or help steer the project forward in any number of ways. ODL will be composed of numerous projects. Each project will have contributors, committers, and one committer elected by their peers to be the project lead. The initial TSC and project leads will be composed of the experts who developed the code that has been originally contributed to the project. This ensures that the community gets access to the experts most familiar with the contributed code to ramp up and provide mentorship to new community participants. Among initial bootstrap projects, the ODL controller is one of the early projects, which we will introduce in the next section, and then we'll set up our environment for ODL-based Net App development.

The first release from the ODL community was codenamed Hydrogen in February 2014 and it came with an open controller, a virtual overlay network, and protocol plugins and switch device enhancements. Carbon, which is the sixth edition, was released in May 2017 and places more focus on IoT, Metro Ethernet, an improved integration with the OpenStack project, and also **Security, Scale, Stability and Performance (S3P)**. It is a major driver for SDN and orchestration implementation in networks.

Ryu

Ryu originates from a Japanese word meaning flow. It is a component-based, open source SDN framework fully written in Python that provides a precise software component and comprehensive API essential for the development of network applications for control and management.

Ryu supports various protocols for managing network devices, such as OpenFlow, **Network Configuration Protocol (NETCONF)**, and the **OpenFlow Management and Configuration Protocol (OF-Config)**, **Open vSwitch Database (OVSDB)** management protocol. It currently supports OpenFlow versions 1.0, 1.2, 1.3, 1.4, and 1.5 and Nicira extensions. NTT labs currently supports the Ryu controller, and it is also deployed across its various cloud data centers.

Ryu architecture

The following components make up the Ryu architecture.

Ryu libraries

Ryu consists of a wide range of libraries that support southbound protocols and packet processing. Some of the southbound protocols include:

- OF-Config, which is a protocol designed for OpenFlow switch management. It performs a collection of the settings and status of the logical switches, ports, and queues.
- XFlow, which consists of NetFlow and sFlow. sFlow is primarily used to parse an sFlow packet from Open vSwitch. NetFlow and sFlow protocols are primarily network traffic management tools used for packet sampling and aggregation.
- OVSDB, which is primarily used to permit remote management of network nodes.

The Ryu packet library helps you to parse and build various protocol packets, such as VLAN, **Multiprotocol Label Switching (MPLS)**, and **Generic Routing Encapsulation (GRE)**.

Third-party libraries also do exist. The Oslo configuration library (`ryu.contrib.oslo.config`) is one example which is used for the configuration of files and the command-line interface of the Ryu manager.

OpenFlow protocol and controller

Ryu supports the OpenFlow protocol up to the latest version 1.5, and it includes an OpenFlow protocol encoder and decoder library (`ryu.ofproto.ofproto_v1_5_parser`).

Also, a key component of the Ryu architecture is the OpenFlow controller, which comprises:

- `ryu.controller.controller`: Responsible for managing connections from the OpenFlow switches, and also used to manage events that are generated and route events to the appropriate entities such as Ryu applications.
- `ryu.controller.dpset`: Used specifically for the management of the switches. It is to be replaced by `ryu/topology`.
- `ryu.controller.ofp_event`: Used to define OpenFlow events.
- `ryu.controller.ofp_handler`: Used for OpenFlow handling, such as OpenFlow version support negotiation.

Managers and core processes

The Ryu manager is the main executable. It primarily loads and manages all Ryu applications. It listens to the specified IP address and the specified port (6633 by default), allowing any OpenFlow switch (hardware, Open vSwitch, or OVS) to connect.

The app manager is the foundational component for all Ryu applications, and the applications are inherited from its `RyuApp` class. It is also responsible for the routing of messages between various Ryu applications. The core-process component in the architecture includes event management, messaging, in-memory state management, and so on.

Northbound

Ryu comprises a web server function synonymous with **Web Server Gateway Interface (WSGI)**, which acts as an interface that can be used to introduce newer REST APIs into an application. Some of the northbound APIs are:

- `ofctl_rest.py`, which presents a set REST API for updating and collecting switch statistics
- `rest_conf_switch.py`, which is centered around APIs for the switch configuration
- `rest_topology.py`, centered around the link configuration

- `rest.py`, which provides a set of REST APIs for network registration and management of the endpoint (primarily MAC address and OpenFlow port number)
- `rest_nw_id.py`, used to know the specific port which is reserved or used for GRE
- `rest_router.py`, used for obtaining, modifying, or deleting address data and routing data

Applications

Ryu comes with applications such as `simple_switch`, router, isolation, firewall, GRE tunnel, topology, and VLAN. It's applications are single-threaded entities which implement various functionalities in Ryu; they also send asynchronous events to each other.

Ryu applications consist of a receive queue for events, which is in a **first in first out** (**FIFO**) buffer architecture to keep the operation of events. Also, applications include a thread for processing events from this queue; events are released from the receive queue and the right event handler is called. The event handler is called within the context of the event-processing thread, which works in a way that once control is given to the handler, no other events for the Ryu application will be processed until control is returned.

The functional architecture of a Ryu application is shown as follows:

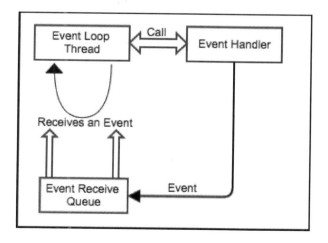

Installation of a Ryu controller

The Ryu controller can be installed easily using various methods:

- Using `pip install`:

  - `sudo pip install -U netaddr six pbr`
  - `pip install ryu`

- Native install from the source code:

  - `git clone git://github.com/osrg/ryu.git`
  - `cd ryu`
  - `sudo python setup.py install`

- Using the Installhelper:

  - `git clone https://github.com/sdnds-tw/ryuInstallhelper.git`
  - `cd ryuInstallHelper`
  - `./ryuInstallHelper.sh`

Running a Ryu application

Ryu applications are basically Python modules that define a subclass of `ryu.base.app_manager.RyuApp`. Two or more classes could be defined in a single module but priority is given to the first module sorted by name order and this is processed by the app manager. One instance of any Ryu application can run at a time in an environment. To run an application in the environment, you need to run the following script:

```
% ryu-manager MyFirstApplication.py
where MyFirstApplication refers to the application name which works as a
simple Layer Two switch.
```

The application can be found as follows:

```
from ryu.base import app_manager
from ryu.controller import ofp_event
from ryu.controller.handler import MAIN_DISPATCHER
from ryu.controller.handler import set_ev_cls
class MyFirstApplication(app_manager.RyuApp):
        def __init__(self, *args, **kwargs):
    super(MyFirstApplication, self).__init__(*args, **kwargs)
        @set_ev_cls(ofp_event.EventOFPPacketIn, MAIN_DISPATCHER)
```

```
        def packet_in_handler(self, ev):
    msg = ev.msg
    dp = msg.datapath
    ofp = dp.ofproto
    ofp_parser = dp.ofproto_parser

    actions = [ofp_parser.OFPActionOutput(ofp.OFPP_FLOOD)]
    out = ofp_parser.OFPPacketOut(
            datapath=dp, buffer_id=msg.buffer_id, in_port=msg.in_port,
actions=actions)
    dp.send_msg(out)
```

A Ryu application raises an event or receives an event. To raise events, the Ryu application calls the appropriate `ryu.base.app_manager.RyuApp` methods, such as the `send_event` or `send_event_to_observers` APIs.

A Ryu application can register itself to listen for specific events using the `ryu.controller.handler.set_ev_cls` decorator. This decorator tells Ryu when the decorated function should be called.

The first argument for the `set_ev_cls` decorator indicates the event of interest, which triggers the following function call, allowing the function to be called every time Ryu receives a `packet_in` message.

The second argument indicates the state of the switch. In a scenario where you need the application to ignore `packet_in` messages before the negotiation between the Ryu controller and the switch finishes, it can use `MAIN_DISPATCHER` as the second argument, which indicates that the following function is called only after the negotiation has been completed.

In our example, our application is interested in `packet_in` events, and every time the Ryu controller gets a `packet_in` message, a handler function should be called. In addition, our application is able to send a received packet to all ports.

Take a look at the first half of the `packet_in_handler` function:

```
ev.msg is an object that represents a packet_in data structure.
msg.dp is an object that represents a datapath (switch).
dp.ofproto and dp.ofproto_parser are objects that represent the OpenFlow
protocol that Ryu and the switch negotiated.
```

And here is the second half:

- The `OFPActionOutput` class is used with a `packet_out` message to specify a switch port that you want to send the packet out of. In our case, the application needs to send out from all the ports of the switch, so `OFPP_FLOOD` constant is used.
- The `OFPPacketOut` class is used to build a `packet_out` message.
- If you call datapath class's `send_msg` method with a with an OpenFlow message class object, the controller builds the message and sends the on-wire data format to the switch.

Special controllers

In addition to the OpenFlow controllers that we introduced in this chapter, there are also two special-purpose OpenFlow controllers: FlowVisor and RouteFlow. The former acts as a transparent proxy between OpenFlow switches and multiple OpenFlow controllers. It is able to create network slices and can delegate control of each slice to a different OpenFlow controller.

FlowVisor also isolates these slices from each other by enforcing proper policies. RouteFlow, on the other hand, provides virtualized IP routing over OpenFlow-capable hardware. RouteFlow can be considered as a network application on top of OpenFlow controllers. It is composed of an OpenFlow Controller application, an independent server, and a virtual network environment that reproduces the connectivity of a physical infrastructure and runs the IP routing engines.

The routing engines generate the **Forwarding Information Base (FIB)** into the Linux IP tables according to the configured routing protocols (for example, OSPF and BGP). These special controllers are presented in more detail in the further chapters.

Summary

The OpenFlow controller provides the interfaces to the OpenFlow switches on one side and the required API for the development of Net Apps.

In this chapter, the overall functionality of OpenFlow (SDN) controllers were presented and some of the existing implementations (NOX/POX, NodeFlow, and Floodlight) were explained in more detail. NOX was the first OpenFlow controller written in Python and C++. POX is a general, open-source SDN controller written in Python. A learning Ethernet switch Net App, based on the API of POX, was presented. NodeFlow is an OpenFlow controller written in JavaScript for Node.js.

Floodlight is a Java-based OpenFlow controller, based on the Beacon implementation, that works with physical and virtual OpenFlow switches. FlowVisor and RouteFlow as special controllers were also presented in this chapter.

Now, we have covered all the required material in order to set up our SDN/OpenFlow development environment. In the next chapter, this environment will be set up.

5
Setting Up the Environment

In the previous chapters, we introduced the OpenFlow switch and controllers, and in this chapter, we will complete and set up the infrastructure and environment for **network application (Net App)** development. We start with our OpenFlow laboratory based on Mininet and remote OpenFlow controllers (POX), and then we introduce the **OpenDaylight (ODL)** project and its bootstrap project ODL controller as a **Software-Defined Networking (SDN)** controller platform (with OpenFlow support) that can be used for our Net App development.

Specifically, we will cover the following topics:

- Understanding the OpenFlow laboratory
- ODL
- SDN Hub starter VM kit

Understanding the OpenFlow laboratory

In Chapter 3, *Implementing the OpenFlow Switch*, we introduced the Mininet network emulation platform as an OpenFlow laboratory. In this section, we present this laboratory in more detail as it is going to be part of our development environment. Mininet uses lightweight virtualization in the Linux kernel to make a single system look like a complete network. A Mininet host behaves just like a real machine; you can establish an SSH session into it (if you start up an SSH daemon and bridge the network to your host) and run arbitrary programs (anything that runs on Linux is available for you to run, from web servers to Wireshark to Iperf). However, Mininet uses a single Linux kernel for all virtual hosts; this means that you can't run software that depends on BSD, Windows, or other operating systems.

Currently, Mininet supports **Network Address Translation (NAT)** by default using the mn --nat command.

This allows your virtual hosts to communicate with the internet. The NAT reroutes traffic originating at your Mininet server or VM and destined for Mininet's IP subnet (10.0.0.0/8 by default) to the Mininet network, which can break connectivity if you are using addresses in the same range in your LAN.

Furthermore, Mininet hosts (that is, virtual hosts) share the host filesystem and **process ID (PID)** space. This means that you have to be careful if you are running daemons that require configuration in /etc. You also need to be careful not to kill the wrong processes by mistake.

Mininet utilizes specific features built into the Linux operating system that allow a single system to be split into a bunch of smaller containers, each with a fixed share of the processing power, combined with a virtual link code that allows links (for example, Ethernet connections) with accurate delays and speeds (for example, 100 Mbps or 1 Gbps). Internally, Mininet employs lightweight virtualization features in the Linux kernel, including process groups, CPU bandwidth isolation, and network namespaces, and combines them with link schedulers and virtual Ethernet links. A virtual host in Mininet is a group of user-level processes moved into a network namespace (a container for network state). Network namespaces provide process groups with exclusive ownership of interfaces, ports, and routing tables (such as ARP and IP). The data rate of each emulated Ethernet link in Mininet is enforced by Linux traffic control, which has a number of packet schedulers to shape traffic to a configured rate. Mininet allows you to set link parameters, and these can even be set automatically from the command line:

```
$ sudo mn --link tc,bw=10,delay=10ms
mininet> iperf
...
mininet> h1 ping -c10 h2
```

This will set the bandwidth of the links to 10 Mbps and a delay of 10 ms. Given this delay value, the **round trip time (RTT)** should be about 40 ms, since the ICMP request traverses two links (one to the switch, one to the destination) and the ICMP reply traverses two links coming back.

You can customize each link using the Python API of Mininet: https://github.com/mininet/mininet/wiki/Introduction-to-Mininet.

Each virtual host has its own virtual Ethernet interface(s). A virtual Ethernet pair acts like a wire connecting two virtual interfaces, or virtual switch ports: packets sent through one interface are delivered to the other, and each interface appears as a fully functional Ethernet port to all system and application software. Mininet typically uses the default Linux bridge or Open vSwitch running in kernel mode to switch packets across the interfaces, as shown in the following diagram:

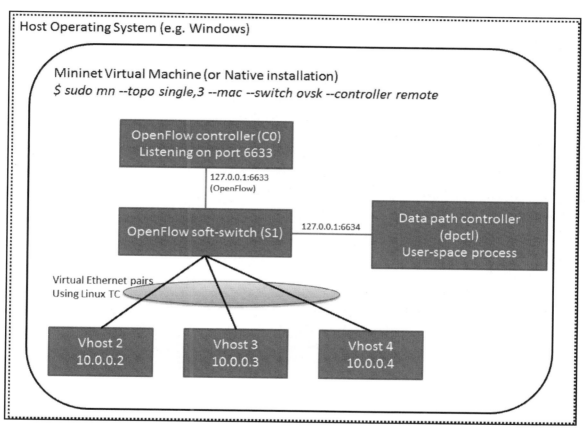

A sample experimental network inside the OpenFlow Laboratory

The preceding diagram presents the virtual hosts, soft switch, and the OpenFlow controller, which are created inside the Mininet Linux server (or Mininet Linux VM image). To create this network topology, you can simply enter the following command in an SSH terminal:

```
$ sudo mn --topo single,3 --mac --switch ovsk --controller remote
```

This command line instructs Mininet to start up a three-host, single-switch (Open vSwitch-based) topology, set the MAC address of each host equal to its IP address, and point to a remote controller, which defaults to the localhost. Each virtual host has its own separate IP address. A single OpenFlow soft-switch in the kernel with three ports is also created. Virtual hosts are connected to the soft-switch with virtual Ethernet links (for example, cables). The MAC address of each host is set to its IP address. Finally, the OpenFlow soft-switch is connected to a remote controller.

 The examples directory (`~/mininet/examples`) in the Mininet source tree includes examples of how to use Mininet's Python API, and potentially useful code that has not been integrated into the main code base of Mininet.

In addition to the mentioned components, `dpctl` is a utility that comes with the OpenFlow reference distribution and enables visibility and control over a single switch's flow table. It is especially useful for debugging purposes and to provide visibility over flow state and flow counters. To obtain this information you can poll the switch on port `6634`. The following command in an SSH window connects to the switch and dumps out its port state and capabilities:

```
$ dpctl show tcp:127.0.0.1:6634
```

The following command dumps the flow table of the soft-switch:

```
$ dpctl dump-flows tcp:127.0.0.1:6634
stats_reply (xid=0x1b5ffa1c): flags=none type=1(flow) cookie=0,
duration_sec=1538s, duration_nsec=567000000s, table_id=0,
priority=500, n_packets=0, n_bytes=0,
idle_timeout=0,hard_timeout=0,in_port=1,actions=output:2
cookie=0, duration_sec=1538s, duration_nsec=567000000s,
table_id=0, priority=500, n_packets=0,
n_bytes=0,idle_timeout=0,hard_timeout=0,in_port=2,
actions=output:1
```

You can also use `dpctl` to manually install the necessary flows. For example:

```
$ dpctl add-flow tcp:127.0.0.1:6634 in_port=1,actions=output:2
$ dpctl add-flow tcp:127.0.0.1:6634 in_port=2,actions=output:1
```

It will forward packets coming at port 1 to port 2 and vice versa. This can be checked by dumping the flow table:

```
$ dpctl dump-flows tcp:127.0.0.1:6634
```

By default, Mininet runs Open vSwitch in OpenFlow mode, which requires an OpenFlow controller. Mininet comes with built-in `Controller()` classes to support several controllers, including the OpenFlow reference controller (`controller`), Open vSwitch's OVS controller, and the now-deprecated NOX Classic. You can simply choose which OpenFlow controller you want when you invoke the `mn` command:

```
$ sudo mn --controller ref
$ sudo mn --controller ovsc
$ sudo mn --controller NOX,pyswitch
```

Each of these examples uses a controller which turns your OVS switch into an Ethernet learning switch.

> `ovsc` is easy to install, but only supports 16 switches. You can install the reference controller using `install.sh -f`. You can also install NOX Classic using `install.sh -x`, but note that NOX Classic is deprecated and may not be supported in the future.

External controllers

When you start a Mininet network, each switch can be connected to a remote controller, which could be in the Mininet VM, outside the Mininet VM, and on your local machine, or in principle anywhere in the internet. This setup may be convenient if you already have a controller framework and development tool installed on the localhost or you want to test a controller running on a different physical machine. If you want to try this, you have to make sure that your controller is reachable from the Mininet VM and fill in the host IP and/or listening port:

```
$ sudo mn --controller=remote,ip=[controller IP],port=[controller
listening port]
```

For instance, to run POX's sample learning switch, you could do something like this in one window:

```
$ cd ~/pox
$ ./pox.py forwarding.l2_learning
```

In another window, start up Mininet to connect to the remote controller (which is actually running locally, but outside of Mininet's control):

```
$ sudo mn --controller=remote,ip=127.0.0.1,port=6633
```

 Note that these are actually the default IP address and port values. If you generate some traffic (`mininet> h1 ping h2`) you should be able to observe some output in the POX window showing that the switch has connected and that some flow table entries have been installed.

Completing the OpenFlow laboratory

Our OpenFlow laboratory consists of four key building blocks:

- Virtualization software, for example, VirtualBox or VMware Player, to host the Mininet VM
- A terminal program with SSH support, for example, PuTTY
- An X Server for X11 forwarding, for example, Xming or XQuartz
- The Mininet (2.0) VM image

The following diagram shows the complete building blocks and setup of the OpenFlow laboratory that will be used for Net App development. A number of OpenFlow (and SDN) controller frameworks are readily available and should work with Mininet as long as you start them up and specify the remote controller option with the correct IP address of the host where your controller is located and the correct port that it is listening on. In any case, you have to make sure that your Mininet hosts have proper internet access.

If you are running VirtualBox, you should make sure your VM has two network interfaces. One should be a NAT interface that can be used to access the internet, and the other should be a host-only interface to enable it to communicate with the host machine. For example, your NAT interface could be **eth0** and have a **10.x** IP address, and your host-only interface could be **eth1** and have a **192.168.x** IP address:

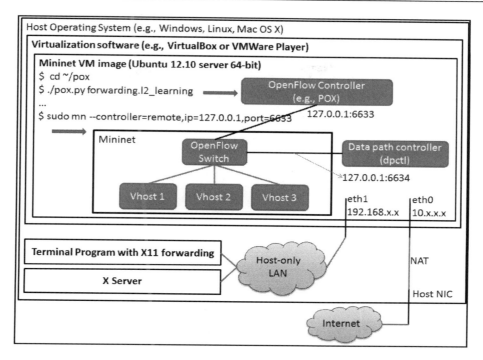

The OpenFlow laboratory environment and building blocks

 In VirtualBox, you should put the second network interface in host-only mode. Select your VM image and go to the **Settings** tab and then to **Network Adapter 2**. Select the **Enable adapter** box, and attach it to **Host-only network**. This will allow you to easily access your VM through your host machine.

Now, you have to verify that you can connect from the host PC (your laptop) to the guest VM (OpenFlow laboratory) via SSH. From the virtual machine console, log in to the VM (username: `mininet`, password: `mininet`), and then enter the following command:

```
$ ifconfig -a
```

You should see three interfaces (`eth0`, `eth1`, `lo`), and both `eth0` and `eth1` should have IP addresses assigned. If this is not the case, type the following:

```
$ sudo dhclient ethX
```

Replacing ethX with the name of the unnumbered interface

Note down the IP address of `eth1` (probably the `192.168.x.x` one) for the host-only network; you will need it later. Next, using your SSH client (PuTTY, terminal.app, and so on) log in to your Mininet VM. For example, on a Linux host, enter the following command:

```
$ ssh -X mininet@[eth1's IP address]
```

In order to use the X11 applications (xterm and Wireshark), the X Server must be running. The next verification is the accessibility of the X server. Try starting up an X terminal using the `xterm` command:

```
$ xterm
```

Then a new terminal window should appear. If you have succeeded, the environment of the OpenFlow laboratory will be ready and you can close the xterm. If you get an `xterm: Xt error: Can't open display` (or similar error), verify your X server installation.

Under Windows, the Xming server must be running, and you must make an SSH connection with X11 forwarding enabled. First, start Xming. Xming will not show any window, but you can verify that it is running by looking for its process in Windows' taskbar. Second, make an SSH connection with X11 forwarding enabled. If you are using PuTTY, you can connect to your OpenFlow laboratory by entering your VM's IP address (`eth1`) and enabling X11 forwarding. To enable X11 forwarding from PuTTY's GUI, open PuTTY and go to **Connection | SSH | X11**, then enable X11 forwarding.

Alternatively, you can install X11 into the VM itself (that is, inside your OpenFlow laboratory VM). To install X11 and a simple window manager, log in to the VM console window (username: `mininet`, password: `mininet`) and enter the following commands:

```
$ sudo apt-get update
$ sudo apt-get install xinit flwm
```

Now, you should be able to start an X11 session in the VM console window by typing this:

```
$ startx
```

After establishing an SSH connection to your OpenFlow laboratory VM and logging in to it (username: `mininet`, password: `mininet`), you can start the sample Mininet network by entering the following command:

```
$ sudo mn --topo single,3 --mac --switch ovsk --controller remote
```

Note that since you have not started any OpenFlow controller, you will get an error message like `unable to contact the remote controller at 127.0.0.1:6633`. Since X11 forwarding is also enabled, you can start Wireshark to be able to capture OpenFlow traffic. You can start Wireshark by entering the following command in your terminal (PuTTY):

```
mininet@mininet-vm:~$ wireshark &
```

This will open the Wireshark GUI and you can start capturing the network traffic and filtering the OpenFlow traffic as explained in Chapter 3, *Implementing the OpenFlow Switch*.

Now you can start your remote OpenFlow controller. This controller is in fact running inside your OpenFlow laboratory VM. So you need to go to your VM console and enter the following commands:

```
mininet@mininet-vm:~$ cd pox
mininet@mininet-vm:~/pox$ ./pox.py forwarding.l2_learning
```

After a while your OpenFlow soft-switch in the Mininet will get connected to this controller. The output of your POX controller should look like the following:

```
POX 0.0.0 / Copyright 2011 James McCauley
DEBUG:core:POX 0.0.0 going up...
DEBUG:core:Running on CPython (2.7.3/Sep 26 2012 21:51:14)
INFO:core:POX 0.0.0 is up.
This program comes with ABSOLUTELY NO WARRANTY.  This program is
free software, and you are welcome to redistribute it under
certain conditions.
Type 'help(pox.license)' for details.
DEBUG:openflow.of_01:Listening for connections on 0.0.0.0:6633
INFO:openflow.of_01:[Con 1/1] Connected to 00-00-00-00-00-01
DEBUG:forwarding.l2_learning:Connection [Con 1/1]
Ready.
POX>
```

The debug messages of POX show that your OpenFlow switch is connected to POX (OpenFlow controller) and behaves as an L2 learning switch.

This concludes the setup of our OpenFlow laboratory. We managed to set up a network using Mininet and also started a remote OpenFlow controller (POX) as an environment for Net App development. In Chapter 6, *Net App Development*, we will use this laboratory setup for our sample Net App development.

In the next section, we'll introduce another setup based on the ODL project.

ODL

ODL is a Linux foundation collaborative project (https://www.opendaylight.org/), in which a community has come together to fill the need for an open and reference framework for programmability and control through an open source SDN solution. It combines open community developers, open source code, and project governance that guarantees an open, community decision-making process on business and technical issues. ODL can be a core component within any SDN architecture.

Building upon an open source SDN controller enables users to reduce operational complexity, extend the lifetime of their existing network infrastructure, and enable new services and capabilities only available with SDN. The mission statement of the ODL project is *"OpenDaylight facilitates a community-led industry-supported open source framework, including code and architecture, to accelerate and advance a common, robust Software-Defined Networking platform."*

ODL is open to anyone. Anyone can develop and contribute code, get elected to the **Technical Steering Committee (TSC)**, get voted onto the board, or help steer the project forward in any number of ways. ODL will be composed of numerous projects. Each project will have contributors, committers, and one committer elected by their peers to be the project lead. The initial TSC and project leads will be composed of the experts who developed the code that has been originally contributed to the project. This ensures the community gets access to the experts most familiar with the contributed code to ramp up and provide mentorship to new community participants.

The ODL controller is one of the early bootstrap projects; we will introduce it in the next section and then we set up our environment for ODL-based Net App development.

ODL controller

The ODL controller is a highly available, modular, extensible, scalable, and multi-protocol controller infrastructure built for SDN deployment on modern heterogeneous multi-vendor networks. The model-driven **Service Abstraction Layer (SAL)** provides the needed abstractions to support multiple southbound protocols (for example, OpenFlow) via plugins. The application-oriented extensible northbound architecture provides a rich set of northbound APIs via RESTful web services for loosely coupled applications and OSGi services for colocated applications.

The OSGi framework, upon which the controller platform is built, is responsible for the modular and extensible nature of the controller and also provides versioning and life-cycle management for OSGi modules and services. The ODL controller supports not only the OpenFlow protocol, but also other open protocols to allow communication with devices that have OpenFlow and/or respective agents. It also includes a northbound API to allow customer applications (software), which will work with the controller in controlling the network.

ODL is developed using Java and as a JVM it can run on any hardware platform and OS, provided it supports Java JVM 1.7 and higher. The architecture of ODL is shown in the following screenshot:

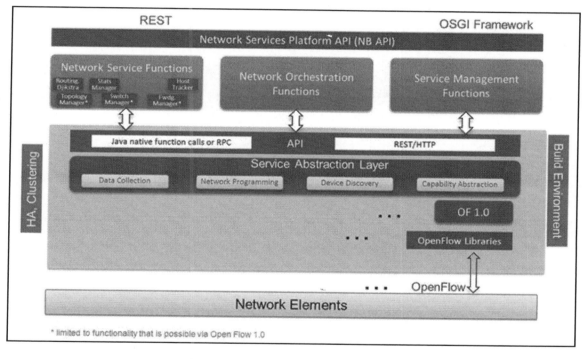

Architecture of ODL Controller

The southbound ODL controller can support multiple protocols as plugins (OpenFlow 1.0, PCE, BGP-LS, and so on). It currently supports OpenFlow 1.0. Other ODL contributors may add to those as part of their contributions/projects. These modules are dynamically linked into an SAL. The SAL exposes services which the modules in the higher layer serve. The SAL figures out how to fulfill the requested service irrespective of the underlying protocol used between the controller and the network elements (OpenFlow switch).

This provides investment protection to the applications as OpenFlow and other protocols evolve over time. The information regarding capabilities and reachability of the network devices is stored and managed by the topology manager. The other components (for example, ARP handler, host tracker, device manager, and switch manager) help in generating the topology database for the topology manager. The switch manager API holds the details of the network element.

As a network element is discovered, its attributes (what switch/router it is, SW version, capabilities, and so on) are stored in the database by the switch manager. The controller exposes open northbound APIs, which are used by the applications. The ODL controller supports the OSGi framework and bidirectional REST for the northbound API. The OSGi framework is used for applications that will run in the same address space as the controller, while the REST (web-based) API is used for apps that do not run in the same address space (or even the same hardware/software platform) as the controller.

The business logic and algorithms reside in the Net Apps. These Net Apps use the controller to gather network intelligence, run its algorithm to perform analytics, and then use the controller to orchestrate the new rules throughout the network. The ODL controller supports a cluster-based high-availability model. There are several instances of the ODL controller, which logically act as one logical controller. This not only gives fine-grained redundancy, but also allows a scale-out model for linear scalability. The ODL controller has a built-in GUI. The GUI is implemented as an application using the same northbound API as would be available for any other user application.

 For more information about the architecture, development infrastructure, library description, and API references, refer to the ODL controller wiki page, which is located at `http://wiki.opendaylight.org/view/OpenDaylight_Controller:Programmer_Guide`.

ODL-based SDN laboratory

In this section, we set up our SDN laboratory (with built-in OpenFlow support) using our ODL controller. Our procedure assumes that you are installing the ODL controller on your local Linux machine and you will use the Mininet VM (as detailed in the previous sections) to create a virtual network. Our host operating system is Windows 7 Enterprise and therefore, throughout this section, we will use VMware Player to host another VM (Ubuntu 12.04) for the ODL controller. The settings of our VM are as follows:

- Two CPUs, 2 GB RAM, and 20 GB disk space.
- Bridged NIC, which puts the VM on the same network as your NIC. You can bind to wireless or wired. So if your physical host, such as your laptop, is on `192.168.0.10/24`, a VM in bridged mode would get `192.168.0.11/24` or whatever your DHCP server assigns to it. The point is to have the VM remain on the same subnet as your host computer.

After logging in to your VM, you have to download the following prerequisite software:

- JVM 1.7 or higher, for example, OpenJDK 1.7 (`JAVA_HOME` should be set to the environment variable)
- Git to pull the ODL controller from the Git repository
- Maven

Install the dependencies and pull down the code using Git:

```
$ sudo apt-get update
$ sudo apt-get install maven git openjdk-7-jre openjdk-7-jdk
$ git clone http://git.opendaylight.org/gerrit/p/controller.git
$ cd controller/opendaylight/distribution/opendaylight/
$ mvn clean install
$ cd target/distribution.opendaylight-0.1.0-SNAPSHOT-
osgipackage/opendaylight
```

This will install the required tools and get the ODL controller from the Git repository. Then Maven will build and install the ODL controller. Apache Maven is a build automation tool used primarily for Java projects. Note that building the ODL controller takes a few minutes.

If your Maven build fails with an `Out Of Memory error: PermGen Space` error, rerun Maven using the `-X` switch to enable full debug logging. This is due to a memory leak somewhere in the Maven build and is being tracked as a bug. Instead of `mvn clean install` you can run `maven clean install -DskipTests` and it will skip the integration tests that seem to be the source of the garbage collector's leak. You can also address this error by setting maven options using `$ export MAVEN_OPTS="-Xmx512m -XX:MaxPermSize=256m` command.

The summary at the end of Maven build will report the successful build of the ODL controller along with the elapsed time and allocated/available memory. Before running the ODL controller, you have to set up the `JAVA_HOME` environment variable. The current value of `JAVA_HOME` can be viewed with the `echo $JAVA_HOME` command. It will likely be undefined. Export the `JAVA_HOME` environment variable. You can write it to `.bashrc` (located in the user home directory) to have it be persistent through reboots and logins. Place `JAVA_HOME=/usr/lib/jvm/java-1.7.0-openjdk-amd64` at the bottom of your `~/.bashrc` file, or for one-time use, set it with the following:

```
$ export JAVA_HOME=/usr/lib/jvm/java-1.7.0-openjdk-i386
(or -amda64)
```

You can start the ODL controller by changing the current directory to the location where the ODL binary is available and start it with `run.sh`:

```
$ cd ~/controller/opendaylight/distribution/opendaylight
/target/distribution.opendaylight-0.1.0-SNAPSHOT-osgipackage
/opendaylight
$ ./run.sh
```

The ODL controller needs a couple of minutes to get all of its modules loaded. You can point your browser to `127.0.0.1:8080` to open the ODL controller web interface (see the following screenshot). The default username and password is `admin` (username: `admin`, password: `admin`):

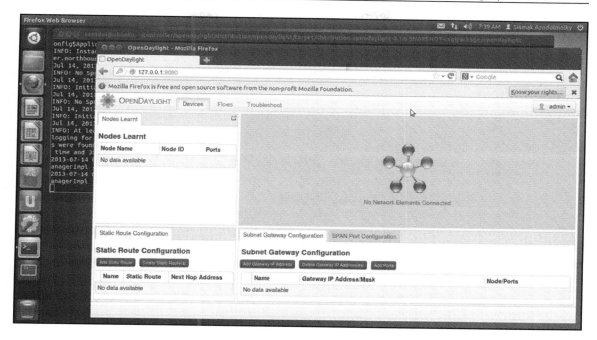

The web-based GUI of the ODL controller

Now that we have the ODL controller up and running, we can point the OpenFlow switch of our OpenFlow laboratory to this controller. The ODL controller has been tested against the Mininet VM, which is part of our OpenFlow laboratory. Launch the Mininet VM with VMware player, VirtualBox, or another virtualization application. Log in to the Mininet VM (username: `mininet`, password: `mininet`). Determine the IP address of the server hosting the ODL controller (for example, $ `ifconfig -a`), and use it to start a virtual network:

```
mininet@mininet-vm:~$ sudo mn --controller=remote,
ip=controller-ip --topo single,3
```

Mininet will connect to the ODL controller and set up a switch and three hosts connected to it, as shown in the following screenshot:

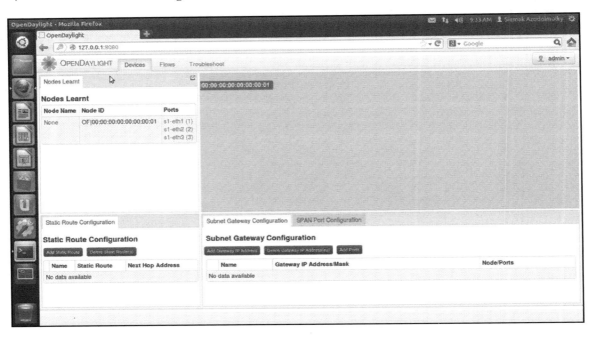

The GUI of the ODL controller after setting up the network in Mininet

When you point an OpenFlow switch at the ODL controller, it will pop up as a device waiting to be configured. The datapath ID is the unique key identifier made up of the switch MAC and an ID assigned by the controller. Mininet will use all zeroes with a 1 at the end. OpenFlow uses LLDP for topology discovery by using the `packet_out` instruction, in which the controller tells the forwarding element to do something like sending an LLDP discovery. Next, specify the action for the **Flow Modification (FlowMod)**.

The following screenshot shows part of a web-based form that collects the parameter for a flow entry, which can be installed in the flow table of OpenFlow switches. Here, we choose the output port. Remember that OpenFlow only forwards what you instruct it to, so either add rules to handle 0×0806 Ethernet-type traffic for ARP broadcast requests and unicast replies or delete the Ethernet-type default IPv4 0×0800 value when you add a FlowMod.

You also need to set up a match on traffic from port 1 with an action to forward to port 2 along with the return traffic of matching port 2 with the output action of port 1. You can specify reserved ports such as normal, controller, flood, and all of the others listed in the drop-down boxes from the OpenFlow v1.0 specification. Choose an action that can be logical or physical. Logical ones tend to be named with a symbolic representation while physical is numeric. Ports are learned by the switch sending configuration information and also updated if a port or link goes down. By adding the proper flows in the flow table of S1, you can establish a path between hosts and check it by pinging those hosts in Mininet. For troubleshooting, you can use dpctl or Wireshark, which was covered earlier in this chapter and also in Chapter 3, *Implementing the OpenFlow Switch*:

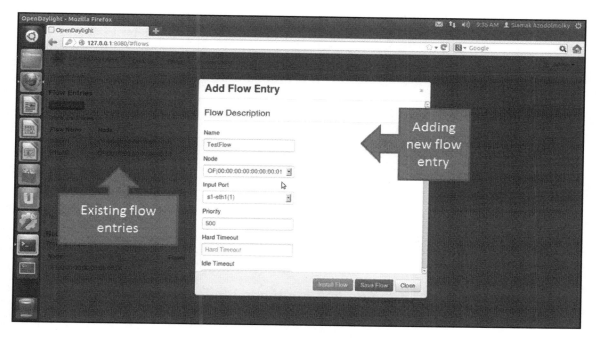

Adding new flow entry dialog box

SDN Hub starter VM kit

SDN Hub created a starter kit tutorial VM, which comprises various components that will facilitate SDN development.

The VM is Ubuntu 64-bit based, which is preinstalled with various software and tools. Some of the tools installed are as follows:

- Controllers: OpenDaylight, ONOS, RYU, Floodlight, Floodlight-OF1.3, POX, and Trema
- Open VSwitch 2.3, which also supports OpenFlow 1.2, 1.3, and 1.4, LINC Switch
- Mininet
- Pyretic
- Wireshark 1.12.1 with native support for OpenFlow parsing
- JDK 1.8, Eclipse Luna, and Maven 3.3

The VM can be downloaded from `https://github.com/PacktPublishing/-Software-Defined-Networking-with-OpenFlow.`

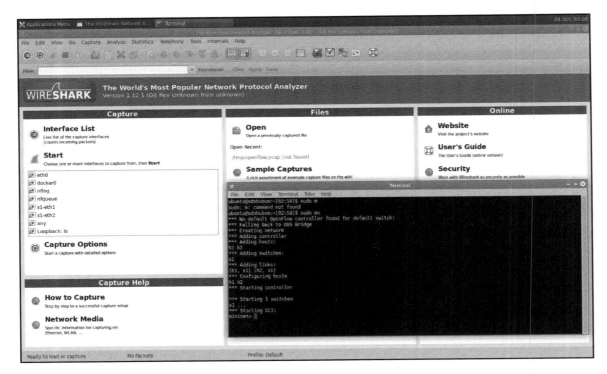

The preceding screenshot shows the layout of the VM with Wireshark open and Mininet started.

The username and password for the VM is Ubuntu. Start your applications such as Wireshark and Mininet using the sudo command, for example, sudo wireshark & and sudo mn.

Summary

In this chapter, we had a detailed description on our OpenFlow laboratory based on Mininet and its role as a network emulator that can be interfaced to remote controllers (POX). This setup is the development infrastructure upon which we can utilize the northbound API of the OpenFlow controllers (for example, POX) to develop Net Apps in the next chapter.

Furthermore, we presented the ODL project and its bootstrap controller (that is, ODL controller), which can be used as an SDN controller for our development environment. The ODL controller and its northbound interface, which was also interfaced to the Mininet network emulator, is another promising environment, which we will use in the next chapter for sample Net App development.

6
Net App Development

Up to this point, we have covered the details of OpenFlow functionalities and the role of OpenFlow switches and OpenFlow controllers in the SDN ecosystem. In Chapter 5, *Setting Up the Environment*, we set up our development environment, and in this chapter, we go through some **network applications (Net Apps)** using the POX OpenFlow controller and also the OpenDaylight controller that we introduced and set up in the previous chapter. Note that the potential and capabilities of OpenFlow controllers are more than the sample Net Apps that we introduce in this chapter. However, the goal here is to give you an initial push toward the basic steps in developing Net Apps using the OpenFlow framework. In the first part of this chapter, we will start with our OpenFlow laboratory (based on Mininet) and will go through the operation of an Ethernet hub, an Ethernet learning switch, and a simple firewall. Then, we will go through the details of a learning switch over the OpenDaylight controller.

Net App 1 - an Ethernet learning switch

Using our Mininet-based OpenFlow laboratory, we are going to set up a simple network consisting of an OpenFlow switch, three hosts, and an OpenFlow controller (POX). The topology of the network is shown in the following diagram:

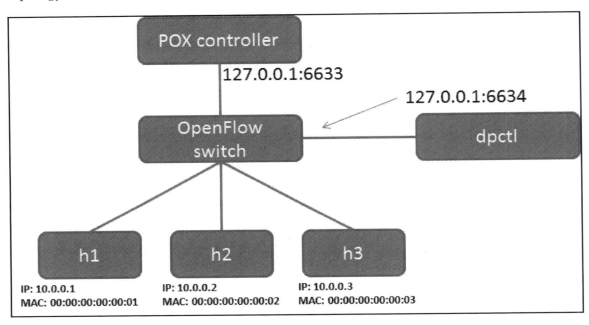

Experimental network topology in our OpenFlow laboratory using Mininet

In addition to the POX controller, we also use the `dpctl` utility program to examine the flow table of the OpenFlow switch. As mentioned earlier, OpenFlow switches usually are listening on port `6634`, which is considered for the `dpctl` channel. Even without an OpenFlow controller, we can use the `dpctl` utility program to communicate with the OpenFlow switch in our OpenFlow laboratory and inspect flow table entries or modify flows. In order to set up the network topology depicted in the previous figure inside our Mininet OpenFlow laboratory, we start Mininet with the following command-line parameters:

```
mininet@mininet-vm:~$ sudo mn --topo single,3 --mac --switch ovsk
--controller remote
```

Note that Mininet reports that it is not able to connect to the remote controller at
`127.0.0.1:6633` (`localhost:6633`).

```
*** Adding controller
Unable to connect the remote controller at 127.0.0.1:6633
```

In fact, since we have not started any POX controller so far, the OpenFlow switch is not able
to connect to the remote controller (as indicated by `--controller remote` in the
command-line parameters of the Mininet launcher). Note that `--controller remote` by
default refers to an OpenFlow controller located on the localhost (`127.0.0.1`). You can
check the IP address and MAC address of `h1` (and other hosts) using the following
command:

```
mininet> h1 ifconfig
```

Now we can try to check the connectivity among the hosts (`h1`, `h2`, and `h3`) using the
`pingall` command of Mininet:

```
mininet> pingall
```

The following will be the output:

```
*** Ping: testing ping reachability
h1 -> X X
h2 -> X X
h3 -> X X
*** Results: 100% dropped (6/6 lost)
```

These results show that the hosts (in spite of being physically connected to each other) in
the current topology are not logically connected (are not reachable) to each other through
the switch due to lack of any flow entry rule in the flow table of the switch. We can dump
the content of the flow table of the OpenFlow switch using the following command (you
need to establish an SSH terminal connection to your Mininet VM to issue this command):

```
mininet@mininet-vm:~$ dpctl dump-flows tcp:127.0.0.1:6634
```

The following will be the output:

```
status reply (xid=0xf36abb08): flags=none type=1 (flow)
```

Before attaching the POX controller to our network topology, in which the controller will play the role of an Ethernet hub, let's quickly review the operation of an Ethernet hub. An Ethernet hub (an active hub or multiport repeater) is a device for connecting multiple Ethernet devices together and making them act as a single network segment. It has multiple input/output ports, in which a signal introduced at the input of any port appears at the output of every port except the original incoming one. No forwarding information is stored in the switch. The hub functionality is implemented in the `hub.py` code of the POX distribution (developed by James McCauley). This program (along with the L2 learning switch) is located in the `~/pox/pox/forwarding` directory. Looking at `hub.py`, we can find the launch method, which simply adds a listener for OpenFlow switches to connect to it:

```
def launch ():
    core.openflow.addlisternetByName("connectionUp", _handle_ConnectionUp)
    log.info("Hub running.")
```

The `_handle_connectionUp` method, which is another method in `hub.py`, simply generates an OpenFlow message for the OpenFlow switch. The action appended to the message simply floods the packet on all ports of the OpenFlow switch (except the incoming port). The generated message is then sent to the OpenFlow switch in our experimental network topology:

```
def _handle_ConnectionUp (event):
    msg= of.ofp_flow_mod()
    msg.actions.append(of.ofp_action_output(port= of.OFPP_FLOOD))
    event.connection.send(msg)
    log.info("Hubifying %s", dpidToStr(event.dpid))
```

So the event handler (`_handle_ConnectionUp`) simply receives an event from the OpenFlow switch and then caches a *flooding* rule inside the flow table of the switch. Let's start the POX controller with the following hub functionality:

```
mininet@mininet-vm:~/pox$ ./pox.py forwarding.hub
```

The following will be the output:

```
POX POX 0.0.0 / Copyright 2011 James McCauley
INFO:forwarding.hub:Hub running.
DEBUG:core:POX 0.0.0 going up...
DEBUG:core:Running on CPython (2.7.3/Sep 26 2012 21:51:14)
INFO:core:POX 0.0.0 is up.
This program comes with ABSOLUTELY NO WARRANTY.  This program is free
software, and you are welcome to redistribute it under certain conditions.
Type 'help(pox.license)' for details.
DEBUG:openflow.of_01:Listening for connections on 0.0.0.0:6633
Ready.
```

```
POX> INFO:openflow.of_01:[Con 1/1] Connected to 00-00-00-00-00-01
INFO:forwarding.hub:Hubifying 00-00-00-00-00-01
```

Note that upon the start of the POX controller (functioning as an Ethernet hub), an information message confirms that the OpenFlow switch is connected to the POX controller. The data path identification (dpid) of the switch is also printed out as 00-00-00-00-00-01. You can return to the Mininet command prompt and issue the net command to see the network elements, in which C0 (controller 0) will be also printed out. Now we can try to ping all hosts in our topology using the pingall command of Mininet:

```
mininet> pingall
```

The following will be the output:

```
*** Ping: testing ping reachability
h1 -> h2 h3
h2 -> h1 h3
h3 -> h1 h2
*** Results: 0% dropped (0/6 lost)
```

And we can also use dpctl (from our new SSH terminal) to see the content of the flow table of our OpenFlow switch:

```
mininet@mininet-vm:~$ dpctl dump-flows tcp:127.0.0.1:6634
```

The following will be the output:

```
stats_reply (xid=0x2f0cd1c7): flags=none type=1(flow)
cookie=0, duration_sec=800s, duration_nsec=467000000s, table_id=0,
priority=32768, n_packets=24, n_bytes=1680, idle_timeout=0,
hard_timeout=0,actions=FLOOD
```

So, we started our experimental network topology in Mininet and made its OpenFlow switch get connected to the POX controller, which was behaving like an Ethernet hub. The interesting point about our first Net App is that just with 12 lines of code in Python (hub.py), we managed to perform the Ethernet hub functionality in the network.

Building the learning switch

Now, we change and enhance the behavior of our OpenFlow switch to an intelligent (learning) Ethernet switch. Let's review the operation of a learning switch. When a packet arrives on any port of the learning switch, it can learn that the sending host is located on the port on which the packet has arrived. So, it can simply maintain a lookup table that associates the MAC address of the host with the port on which they are connected to the switch. So the switch stores the source MAC address of the packet along with the incoming port in its lookup table. Upon receiving a packet, the switch looks up the destination MAC address of the packet; in case of a match, the switch figures out the output port and instead of flooding the packet, it simply sends the packet to its correct destination host (through the looked-up port). In the OpenFlow paradigm, each incoming packet basically generates a new rule in the flow table of the OpenFlow switch. In order to observe this behavior, we restart our experimental network with the 12_learning switch (12_learning.py) functionality. The learning switch algorithm, which is implemented in the 12_learning.py script consists of the following steps:

1. The first step is to use the source MAC address of the packet and the switch port to update the switching lookup table (the address/port table), maintained inside the controller as a hash table.

2. The second step is to drop certain types of the packets (packets with an Ethertype of LLDP or packets with a bridge-filtered destination address).

3. In the third step, the controller checks if the destination address is a multicast address. In that case, the packet is simply flooded.

4. If the destination MAC address of the packet is not already inside the address/port table (the hash table, which is maintained inside the controller), then the controller instructs the OpenFlow switch to flood the packet on all ports (except the incoming one).

5. If the output port is the same as the input port, the controller instructs the switch to drop the packet to avoid loops.

6. Otherwise, the controller sends a flow table entry modification command (flow mod) to the switch, using the source MAC address and corresponding port, which instructs the switch that future packets addressed to that specific MAC address will be sent to the associated output port (rather than flooding).

In order to see the learning switch behavior of our setup, we first clean up the existing setup and start our experimental network again:

```
mininet@mininet-vm:~$ sudo mn -c
... (screen messages are removed)
mininet@mininet-vm:~$ sudo mn --topo single,3 --mac --switch ovsk
--controller remote
```

Now using another SSH terminal, we connect to our Mininet VM and start the POX controller, which executes the Ethernet L2 (layer 2) learning switch algorithm:

```
mininet@mininet-vm:~/pox$ ./pox.py forwarding.l2_learning
```

Upon startup of the POX controller, as in the Ethernet hub case, we can observe that the OpenFlow switch will get connected to the controller. Now if we go back to the Mininet console and issue the `pingall` command, we will see that all hosts are reachable:

```
mininet> pingall
```

The following will be the output:

```
*** Ping: testing ping reachability
h1 -> h2 h3
h2 -> h1 h3
h3 -> h1 h2
*** Results: 0% dropped (0/6 lost)
```

So far, the behavior is like in the Ethernet hub case. However, if we dump the flow table of the switch (using the `dpctl` program), we can observe a bunch of different flow table entries. In fact, the flow table entries show different destination MAC addresses along with the associated output ports that incoming packets addressed to that MAC should be forwarded to. For instance, packets addressed to 00:00:00:00:00:03 will be forwarded to the output port number 3.

```
mininet@mininet-vm:~$ dpctl dump-flows tcp:127.0.0.1:6634
```

The following will be the output:

```
stats_reply (xid=0xababe6ce): flags=none type=1(flow)
cookie=0, duration_sec=7s, duration_nsec=912000000s, table_id=0,
priority=32768, n_packets=1, n_bytes=98,
    idle_timeout=10,hard_timeout=30,icmp,dl_vlan=0xffff,dl_vlan_pcp=0x00,
    dl_src=00:00:00:00:00:02,dl_dst=00:00:00:00:00:03,nw_src=10.0.0.2,nw_
dst=10.0.0.3,nw_tos=0x00,icmp_type=0,icmp_code=0,actions=output:3
...
...
(more entries are not shown)
```

Let's take a look at the Python code (`l2_learning.py`) that implements the Ethernet learning switch functionality. The launch method as usual registers the `l2_learning` object with the core POX controller. Upon being instantiated, the `l2_learning` object adds a listener to ensure that it can handle connection-up events from OpenFlow switches that connect to this controller. This object then instantiates the learning switch object and passes the connection event to that object (see the highlighted code in the following snippet):

```
. . .
. . .
class l2_learning (EventMixin):
  """
  Waits for OpenFlow switches to connect and makes them learning
switches.
  """
  def __init__ (self, transparent):
    self.listenTo(core.openflow)
    self.transparent = transparent

  def _handle_ConnectionUp (self, event):
    log.debug("Connection %s" % (event.connection,))
    LearningSwitch(event.connection, self.transparent)
def launch (transparent=False):
  """
  Starts an L2 learning switch.
  """
  core.registerNew(l2_learning, str_to_bool(transparent))
```

Going through the learning switch object, we can observe that upon instantiation of the address/port, a hash table is created (`self.macToPort= {}`) a listener is registered for the packet-in messages (`connection.addListeners(self)`) and then we can see the packet-in handler method (`_handle_PacketIn (self, event)`). The learning switch algorithm portion of the code is as follows:

```
self.macToPort[packet.src] = event.port
if not self.transparent:
  if packet.type == packet.LLDP_TYPE or
  packet.dst.isBridgeFiltered():
    drop()
    return
  if packet.dst.isMulticast():
    flood()
  else:
    if packet.dst not in self.macToPort:
      log.debug("Port for %s unknown -- flooding" %
      (packet.dst,))
        flood()
```

```
    else:
      port = self.macToPort[packet.dst]
   if port == event.port:
      log.warning("Same port for packet from %s -> %s on %s.
      Drop." %
    (packet.src, packet.dst, port), dpidToStr(event.dpid))
    drop(10)
    return
    log.debug("installing flow for %s.%i -> %s.%i" %
    (packet.src, event.port, packet.dst, port))
    msg = of.ofp_flow_mod()
    msg.match = of.ofp_match.from_packet(packet)
    msg.idle_timeout = 10
    msg.hard_timeout = 30
    msg.actions.append(of.ofp_action_output(port = port))
    msg.buffer_id = event.ofp.buffer_id
   self.connection.send(msg)
```

The first step is to update the address/port hash table (`self.macToPort[packet.src] = event.port`). This will associate the MAC address of the sender to the switch port on which the packet has been received by the switch. Certain types of packet are dropped. Multicast traffic is properly flooded. If the destination of the packet is not available in the address/port hash table, the packet is also flooded. If the input and output ports are the same, then the packet will be dropped to avoid a loop (`if port == event.port:`). Finally, a proper flow table entry gets installed inside the flow table of the OpenFlow switch. In summary, the `l2_learning.py` program implements the required logic and algorithm to change the behavior of our OpenFlow switch to an Ethernet learning switch one. In the next section, we will take one more step toward changing the learning switch to a simple firewall.

Net App 2 - a simple firewall

In this section, we take the learning switch Net App and extend it to make packet forwarding decisions based on simple firewall rules that we install at the OpenFlow controller (POX). We are following two important goals in this Net App development. The first one is to demonstrate how easy it is to change the behavior of the network device (OpenFlow switch) by simply changing the Net App on the OpenFlow controller.

The second goal is to give more information about the POX controller. In our simple firewall Net App, we want the switch to make a drop or forwarding decisions based on the value of the source MAC address of the packets. The experimental network will be the one that is shown in the previous diagram. However, we augment the `l2_learning.py` Net App (L2 learning switch) to perform the functionality of a simple firewall. Therefore, we copy the `l2_learning.py` program with a new name (for instance, `simple_firewall.py`) and add the firewall logic and rules on top of the L2 learning switch intelligence. This extension simply checks the source MAC address of the incoming packets and based on the outcome of comparison with the firewall rules, it will forward or drop the packet. If the controller decides that the packet should be forwarded, then it proceeds to perform the L2 switching functions as earlier. So, the new step after updating the address/port table of the L2 learning switch will be to check the source MAC address of the incoming packet against the firewall rules.

This requires only a few simple additions to the learning switch code. First, we need a hash table to store the (switch, source MAC) pairs. It maps the (switch, source MAC) pair to a `True` or `False` logical value indicating whether the packet should be forwarded or dropped. The controller will decide to drop the incoming packet if there is a firewall entry that maps to `False` (FirewallTable(switch, Source MAC) == False), or if there is no firewall entry for that source MAC address in the firewall hash table. The controller will decide to forward the traffic only if there is a `FirewallTable` entry that maps to `True`. These checks can be added to the learning switch code as follows:

```
. . .
    # Initializing our FirewallTable
    self.firewallTable = {}
    # Adding some sample firewall rules
    self.AddRule('00-00-00-00-00-01',EthAddr('00:00:00:00:00:01'))
    self.AddRule('00-00-00-00-00-01',EthAddr('00:00:00:00:00:03'))
. . .
. . .
    # Check the Firewall Rules
    if self.CheckFirewallRule(dpidstr, packet.src) == False:
      drop()
      return
```

The `CheckFirewallRule` method simply performs the required firewalling operation. Basically, it only returns `True` if the firewall table has a rule for the given source MAC address.

```
# check if the incoming packet is compliant to the firewall rules before
normal proceeding
def CheckFirewallRule (self, dpidstr, src=0):
    try:
```

```
entry = self.firewallTable[(dpidstr, src)]
if (entry == True):
  log.debug("Rule (%s) found in %s: FORWARD",
  src, dpidstr)
else:
  log.debug("Rule (%s) found in %s: DROP",
  src, dpidstr)
return entry
except KeyError:
log.debug("Rule (%s) NOT found in %s: DROP",
src, dpidstr)
return False
```

In this example, the firewall rules are set in a way that only packets from MAC address 00:00:00:00:00:01 and 00:00:00:00:00:03 will be processed and forwarded by the switch, and other traffic is simply dropped. Now we can start Mininet and the POX controller with our firewall Net App as follows:

```
mininet@mininet-vm:~$ sudo mn --topo single,3 --mac --switch ovsk
--controller remote
...
```

Run the following command from another SSH terminal:

```
mininet@mininet-vm:~/pox$ ./pox.py log.level --DEBUG
forwarding.simple_firewall.py
```

Note that we have passed additional command-line parameters to the POX controller to be able to see detailed debugging messages of the POX controller while running our firewall Net App. Since there is no rule in the firewall table that allows h2 to forward its traffic, we should expect that the pingall command confirms this expected behavior:

```
mininet> pingall
```

The following will be the output:

```
*** Ping: testing ping reachability
h1 -> X h3
h2 -> X X
h3 -> h1 X
*** Results: 66% dropped (4/6 lost)
```

We can also see from the POX debugging messages that the controller decided to forward or drop different packets depending on the value of the source MAC address of the incoming packets. It is also interesting to note that when the controller decides to forward a packet, it also caches a rule in the flow table of the OpenFlow switch that allows that packet to be forwarded.

As long as that entry remains in the flow table, all packets that match the flow entry table can continue to be forwarded to the switch. This caching (limited duration of flow entry existence in the flow table of the switch) introduces some performance impact on the switch operation. By caching, we are referring to the availability of a flow entry in the flow table of the switch, which allows the high-speed forwarding of packets without any controller involvement. Forwarding performance is degraded when the first packet of a flow (traffic stream of packets) needs to wait for the forwarding decision of the controller. This effect is usually referred to as the first-packet delay of a flow. Let's have it this way: host 1 pings host 3. From the ping output, we can observe that the first packet is facing high latency since the flow table of the switch is empty and the OpenFlow switch should contact the controller. After caching the instruction in the flow table of the switch, packets are forwarded by the switch. After about 30 seconds, the flow table entry expires and again we observe relatively higher latency between the two end hosts (which are h1 and h3) since once again the traffic is redirected to the controller. Following is the command:

```
mininet> h1 ping h3
```

The following will be the output:

```
PING 10.0.0.3 (10.0.0.3) 56(84) bytes of data.
64 bytes from 10.0.0.3: icmp_req=1 ttl=64 time=38.6 ms
64 bytes from 10.0.0.3: icmp_req=2 ttl=64 time=0.264 ms
64 bytes from 10.0.0.3: icmp_req=3 ttl=64 time=0.056 ms
...
64 bytes from 10.0.0.3: icmp_req=32 ttl=64 time=26.8 ms
64 bytes from 10.0.0.3: icmp_req=33 ttl=64 time=0.263 ms
64 bytes from 10.0.0.3: icmp_req=34 ttl=64 time=0.053 ms
```

Net App 3 - simple forwarding in OpenDaylight

In Chapter 5, *Setting Up the Environment*, we also set up an SDN laboratory based on the OpenDaylight controller. In this section, we'll go through a sample forwarding application, which is available in the OpenDaylight distribution. The OpenDaylight controller includes a Net App called **simple forwarding** that lets you use the basic services for making forwarding decisions and installing flows across all devices on the OpenFlow network. This application discovers the presence of a host via ARP message and installs destination-only or 32 entries across all switches in the network, along with the corresponding output ports towards that host.

Refer to `Chapter 5`, *Setting Up the Environment,* for instructions on setting up the SDN laboratory. However, note that the Mininet network should be set up using the following command:

```
sudo mn --controller=remote,ip=<OpenDaylight IP> --topo tree,3
```

With your OpenDaylight controller and Mininet running as described in the previous chapter, log in to the OpenDaylight web interface. Drag and drop devices to organize the topology into its logical arrangement (the tree topology), and save the configuration. Click on the **Add Gateway IP Address** button and add the IP and subnet of 10.0.0.254/8 (see the following screenshot). This will properly initiate the requests to the OpenFlow controller and will update the flow table of switches accordingly:

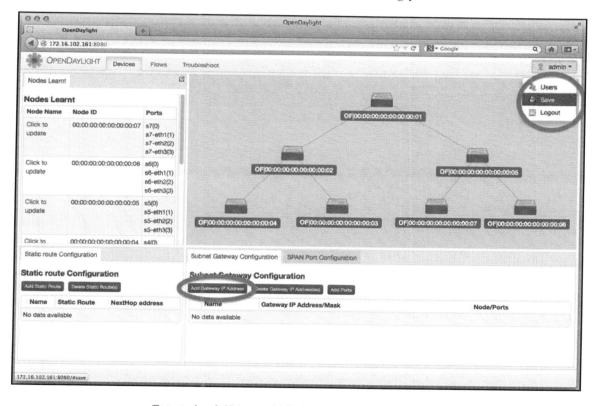

The tree topology of a Mininet network inside the web interface of the OpenDaylight GUI

On the console where Mininet is running, issue the `pingall` command to confirm that all hosts are now reachable from one another. Click on the **Troubleshoot** tab and then load the flow details for one of the switches. View the port details as in the following screenshot:

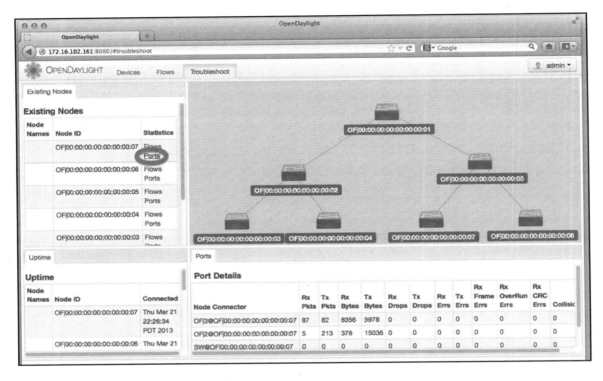

The port details in the OpenDaylight GUI

On the OSGI console (the command-line interface of the console where the ODL controller had been started), type `ss simple`. You will see that the simple forwarding app is ACTIVE, as shown in the following screenshot:

Status of simple forwarding application in the OSGI console

Net App 4 – simple switching hub using Ryu controller

In this section, you will be learning about how a simple switch hub functions based on instructions on the Ryu controller. We shall be using the SDN hub starter kit VM in `Chapter 5`, *Setting Up the Environment,* which has the Ryu controller along with Mininet. The switching hub, which shall be covered in this section, has various capabilities:

- The ability to learn and retain the MAC addresses of hosts connected to any of its ports
- The ability to forward packets to the port of a host whose MAC address has been learned earlier
- The ability to flood packets on all its ports except the incoming ports for packets whose destination MAC address is not present in the MAC address table

In a simple switching hub, the MAC address uses the packet-in function of OpenFlow. This is used by the controller to receive the packet from the switch. These packets are analyzed by the switch where the MAC address is being learned based on the host and the port to which it is connected. Upon analysis, the switch must process the packets based on the MAC address and the MAC address table present in the switch:

- If the destination MAC address is present, the switch uses a packet-out function to forward the packet to the destination host
- If the destination MAC address is not present, flooding is done using the packet-out function

The switching hub can be found in this directory in RYU: `ryu/app/example_switch_13.py`. The simple switch used in this demonstrations supports OpenFlow 1.3.

The switching hub code (`example_switch_13.py`) begins with class definition and initialization:

```
class ExampleSwitch13(app_manager.RyuApp):
OFP_VERSIONS = [ofproto_v1_3.OFP_VERSION]
def __init__(self, *args, **kwargs):
super(ExampleSwitch13, self).__init__(*args, **kwargs)
# initialize mac address table.
self.mac_to_port = {}
```

The `ryu.base.app_manager.RyuApp` is inherited in order to function as a Ryu application. The `ofproto_v1_3.OFP_VERSION` is used to define the OpenFlow 1.3 version.

Next is `mac_to_port`, which defines the MAC address table. Also, `self.mac_to_port =` `{}` defines an empty dictionary that would be used later.

The event handler is then defined and implemented by the Ryu application upon receipt of an OpenFlow message. This event handler defines a function with the event object for the argument and uses the `ryu.controller.handler.set_ev_cls` decorator to decorate. The `set_ev_cls` specifies the event class supporting the received message and the state of the OpenFlow switch for the argument. The event class name is `ryu.controller.ofp_event.EventOFP + < The OpenFlow message name>`. For instance, the packet-in message becomes `EventOFPPacketIn`. Various events listed in the earlier chapters can be substituted here:

```
@set_ev_cls(ofp_event.EventOFPSwitchFeatures, CONFIG_DISPATCHER)
def switch_features_handler(self, ev):
datapath = ev.msg.datapath
ofproto = datapath.ofproto
parser = datapath.ofproto_parser
```

The table-miss flow entry is added to the flow table in preparation to receive the packet-in message once the table-miss flow entry is added upon a handshake with the OpenFlow switch.

The instance of the OpenFlow message class corresponding to the event is stored in `ev.msg`. Here it is `ryu.ofproto.ofproto_v1_3_parser.OFPSwitchFeatures`. In `msg.datapath`, the instance of the `ryu.controller.controller.datapath` class corresponding to the OpenFlow switch that issued this message is stored. Essential processing, such as actual communication with the OpenFlow switch and issuance of the event corresponding to the received message, is performed by the `datapath` class.

The key attributes used by the Ryu applications are as follows:

- The ID that defines the data path ID of the connected OpenFlow switch
- Ofproto, which indicates the `ofproto` module that supports the OpenFlow version, is in use
- `ofproto_parser` defines the `ofproto_parser` module

```
def switch_features_handler(self, ev):
# install the table-miss flow entry.
match = parser.OFPMatch()
actions = [parser.OFPActionOutput(ofproto.OFPP_CONTROLLER,
ofproto.OFPCML_NO_BUFFER)]
self.add_flow(datapath, 0, match, actions)
```

In the instruction of this entry, where the table-miss flow has the lowest priority (0) that matches all the packets and the action is specified to send to the controller port when the packet matches no normal flow entry, the packet-in is issued.

The OFPMatch class is used to match all packets. Transfer to the controller port is done using the output action class, OFPActionOutput. The controller is specified as the output destination and OFPCML_NO_BUFFER is specified to max_len in order for z to send all packets to the controller. Finally, 0 (lowest) is specified for priority and the add_flow() method is executed to send the flow mod message:

```
@set_ev_cls(ofp_event.EventOFPPacketIn, MAIN_DISPATCHER)
def _packet_in_handler(self, ev):
msg = ev.msg
datapath = msg.datapath
ofproto = datapath.ofproto
parser = datapath.ofproto_parser
```

The preceding handler (packet-in event) is used to accept received packets whose MAC address is not known:

```
def _packet_in_handler(self, ev):
# ...
# get the received port number from packet_in message.
in_port = msg.match['in_port']
self.logger.info("packet in %s %s %s %s", dpid, src, dst, in_port)
# learn a mac address to avoid FLOOD next time.
self.mac_to_port[dpid][src] = in_port
# ...
```

The receive port (in_port) is gotten from the OFPPacketIn match, while the sender MAC address and destination MAC address is gotten from the Ethernet header of the received packets using Ryu's packet library.

The MAC address table is then updated based on the port and MAC address of the sender. In order to support connection with multiple OpenFlow switches, the MAC address table is so designed to be managed for each OpenFlow switch. The datapath ID is used to identify the OpenFlow switches:

```
def _packet_in_handler(self, ev):
# ...
# if the destination mac address is already learned,
# decide which port to output the packet, otherwise FLOOD.
if dst in self.mac_to_port[dpid]:
out_port = self.mac_to_port[dpid][dst]
else:
out_port = ofproto.OFPP_FLOOD
```

```
# construct action list.
actions = [parser.OFPActionOutput(out_port)]
# install a flow to avoid packet_in next time.
if out_port != ofproto.OFPP_FLOOD:
match = parser.OFPMatch(in_port=in_port, eth_dst=dst)
self.add_flow(datapath, 1, match, actions)
# ...
```

Based on the preceding portion, an entry is added to the flow table of the OpenFlow switch where the MAC address is found:

```
def add_flow(self, datapath, priority, match, actions):
ofproto = datapath.ofproto
parser = datapath.ofproto_parser
# construct flow_mod message and send it.
inst = [parser.OFPInstructionActions(ofproto.OFPIT_APPLY_ACTIONS,
actions)]
# ...
```

Here, the processing of the packet-in handler occurs.

For flow entries, set a match that indicates the target packet conditions and instructions that indicate the operation on the packet, entry priority level, and effective time:

```
def add_flow(self, datapath, priority, match, actions):
# ...
mod = parser.OFPFlowMod(datapath=datapath, priority=priority,
match=match, instructions=inst)
datapath.send_msg(mod)
```

The entry then needs to be added to the flow table by issuing the flow mod message:

```
def _packet_in_handler(self, ev):
# ...
# construct packet_out message and send it.
out = parser.OFPPacketOut(datapath=datapath,
buffer_id=ofproto.OFP_NO_BUFFER,
in_port=in_port, actions=actions,
data=msg.data)
datapath.send_msg(out)
```

Finally, irrespective of whether the destination MAC address is found from the MAC address table, at the end, the packet-out message is issued and received packets are transferred.

Executing the Simple Switching Hub

For our demonstration, we shall be using the same topology utilized in the previous Net Apps, which have three hosts, one switch, and one controller.

Open a new terminal tab and run the following:

```
$ sudo mn --topo single,3 --mac --switch ovsk --controller remote -x
```

This will create a linear topology and open an xterm to all the devices, as shown in the following screenshot:

The status of the switch can be seen using the `ovs-vsctl show` command, where the OpenFlow version is provided.

Next, we set the OpenFlow version to version 1.3 using `ovs-vsctl set Bridge s1 protocols=OpenFlow13`.

Next, we execute the Ryu Controller on the xterm of the controller (C0) based on the switching hub using the following command:

```
ryu-manager --verbose ryu.app.example_switch_13
```

The following is the screenshot for this:

```
root@sdnhubvm:~[00:52]$ sudo ryu-manager --verbose ryu.app.example_switch_13
/usr/lib/python2.7/dist-packages/pkg_resources.py:1031: UserWarning: /home/ubuntu/.python-eggs is writable by group/others an
d vulnerable to attack when used with get_resource_filename. Consider a more secure location (set with .set_extraction_path o
r the PYTHON_EGG_CACHE environment variable).
  warnings.warn(msg, UserWarning)
loading app ryu.app.example_switch_13
loading app ryu.controller.ofp_handler
instantiating app ryu.app.example_switch_13 of ExampleSwitch13
instantiating app ryu.controller.ofp_handler of OFPHandler
BRICK ExampleSwitch13
  CONSUMES EventOFPPacketIn
  CONSUMES EventOFPSwitchFeatures
BRICK ofp_event
  PROVIDES EventOFPPacketIn TO {'ExampleSwitch13': set(['main'])}
  PROVIDES EventOFPSwitchFeatures TO {'ExampleSwitch13': set(['config'])}
  CONSUMES EventOFPPortDescStatsReply
  CONSUMES EventOFPHello
  CONSUMES EventOFPPortStatus
  CONSUMES EventOFPSwitchFeatures
  CONSUMES EventOFPErrorMsg
  CONSUMES EventOFPEchoRequest
  CONSUMES EventOFPEchoReply
connected socket:<eventlet.greenio.base.GreenSocket object at 0x7fe695e2fe10> address:('127.0.0.1', 37363)
hello ev <ryu.controller.ofp_event.EventOFPHello object at 0x7fe695dc1290>
move onto config mode
EVENT ofp_event->ExampleSwitch13 EventOFPSwitchFeatures
switch features ev version=0x4,msg_type=0x6,msg_len=0x20,xid=0x31061b54,OFPSwitchFeatures(auxiliary_id=0,capabilities=79,data
path_id=1,n_buffers=256,n_tables=254)
move onto main mode
```

Now we have to confirm that the table-miss flow entry has been added to the switch 1 (s1)

```
"switch: s1" (root)
root@sdnhubvm:~[01:17]$ ovs-ofctl -O openflow13 dump-flows s1
OFPST_FLOW reply (OF1.3) (xid=0x2):
 cookie=0x0, duration=1490.898s, table=0, n_packets=0, n_bytes=0, priority=0 actions=CONTROLLER:65535
root@sdnhubvm:~[01:17]$
```

Testing application

In order to test the application, we will have to execute a ping from the host 1 to host 3. The following sequence of events will take place once you send the ping request from host 1 to host 3:

- **ARP request**: An address resolution needs to occur because host 1 does not have knowledge of host 3 MAC's address. Therefore, there is an ARP request broadcast from host 1, which is received by host 2 and host 3.
- **ARP reply**: An ARP reply is sent from host 3 to host 1.

- **ICMP echo request**: Host 1 then sends an echo request to host 3 because it knows the MAC address of host 3.
- **ICMP echo reply**: Host 3 also knows the MAC address of host 1; therefore, an echo reply is sent from host 3 to host 1.

In order to understand the packets received by each host in the topology, it is required that we run the `tcpdump` command:

- **Host 1:** `tcpdump -en -i h1-eth0`
- **Host 2:** `tcpdump -en -i h2-eth0`
- **Host 3:** `tcpdump -en -i h3-eth0`

The result should be in the following format:

```
"host: h3"                                                          — + ⊗
root@sdnhubvm:~[01:58]$ tcpdump -en -i h3-eth0
tcpdump: verbose output suppressed, use -v or -vv for full protocol decode
listening on h3-eth0, link-type EN10MB (Ethernet), capture size 65535 bytes
```

Next, we ping from host 1 toward host 3:

```
mininet> h1 ping -c1 h3
PING 10.0.0.3 (10.0.0.3) 56(84) bytes of data.
64 bytes from 10.0.0.3: icmp_seq=1 ttl=64 time=10.4 ms
--- 10.0.0.3 ping statistics ---
1 packets transmitted, 1 received, 0% packet loss, time 0ms
rtt min/avg/max/mdev = 10.417/10.417/10.417/0.000 ms
mininet>
```

From the preceding result, we can see that the ICMP request has returned successfully. We will then check the flow table of the switch (`s1`):

```
"switch: s1" (root)
root@sdnhubvm:~[02:12]$ ovs-ofctl -O openflow13 dump-flows s1
OFPST_FLOW reply (OF1.3) (xid=0x2):
 cookie=0x0, duration=215.155s, table=0, n_packets=2, n_bytes=140, priority=1,in_port=3,dl_dst=00:00:00:00:00:01 actions=output:1
 cookie=0x0, duration=215.151s, table=0, n_packets=1, n_bytes=42, priority=1,in_port=1,dl_dst=00:00:00:00:00:03 actions=output:3
 cookie=0x0, duration=4793.205s, table=0, n_packets=3, n_bytes=182, priority=0 actions=CONTROLLER:65535
root@sdnhubvm:~[02:12]$ ^C
root@sdnhubvm:~[02:13]$
```

From the preceding screenshot, we can see two new flow entries of priority level 1, which have been registered:

- Receive port `in_port=3`, destination MAC address `dl_dst=00:00:00:00:00:01`, `actions=output:1`.
- Receive port `in_port=1`, destination MAC address `dl_dst=00:00:00:00:00:03`, `actions=output:3`.

From the preceding screenshot, the first entry appeared twice: `{n_packet=2}`. It comprised communication from host 3 to host 1, which is the ARP reply and ICMP echo reply. The second entry is one, which comprises the ARP request that was broadcast from host 1.

Next, we will look at the output of `example_switch_13` running on the Ryu controller:

```
EVENT ofp_event->ExampleSwitch13 EventOFPPacketIn
packet in 1 00:00:00:00:00:01 ff:ff:ff:ff:ff:ff 1
EVENT ofp_event->ExampleSwitch13 EventOFPPacketIn
packet in 1 00:00:00:00:00:03 00:00:00:00:00:01 3
EVENT ofp_event->ExampleSwitch13 EventOFPPacketIn
packet in 1 00:00:00:00:00:01 00:00:00:00:00:03 1
```

From the preceding log, we notice that there are three events logged:

- ARP request where host 1 (`00:00:00:00:00:01`) sends a broadcast (`ff:ff:ff:ff:ff:ff`).
- ARP reply from host 3 (`00:00:00:00:00:03`) to host 1 (`00:00:00:00:00:01`) ICMP echo request from host 1 to host 3.
- Finally, we will look at `tcpdump` of all the hosts.

Host 1 broadcasts the ARP request first and then receives the ARP reply returned from host 3. After this, host 1 issues the ICMP echo request and receives the ICMP echo reply returned from host 3, as shown in the following screenshot:

```
root@sdnhubvm:~[00:50]$ tcpdump -en -i h1-eth0
tcpdump: verbose output suppressed, use -v or -vv for full protocol decode
listening on h1-eth0, link-type EN10MB (Ethernet), capture size 65535 bytes
02:08:58.978415 00:00:00:00:00:01 > ff:ff:ff:ff:ff:ff, ethertype ARP (0x0806), l
ength 42: Request who-has 10.0.0.3 tell 10.0.0.1, length 28
02:08:58.984576 00:00:00:00:00:03 > 00:00:00:00:00:01, ethertype ARP (0x0806), l
ength 42: Reply 10.0.0.3 is-at 00:00:00:00:00:03, length 28
02:08:58.984614 00:00:00:00:00:01 > 00:00:00:00:00:03, ethertype IPv4 (0x0800),
length 98: 10.0.0.1 > 10.0.0.3: ICMP echo request, id 23795, seq 1, length 64
02:08:58.988790 00:00:00:00:00:03 > 00:00:00:00:00:01, ethertype IPv4 (0x0800),
length 98: 10.0.0.3 > 10.0.0.1: ICMP echo reply, id 23795, seq 1, length 64
02:09:04.003208 00:00:00:00:00:03 > 00:00:00:00:00:01, ethertype ARP (0x0806), l
ength 42: Request who-has 10.0.0.1 tell 10.0.0.3, length 28
02:09:04.003224 00:00:00:00:00:01 > 00:00:00:00:00:03, ethertype ARP (0x0806), l
ength 42: Reply 10.0.0.1 is-at 00:00:00:00:00:01, length 28
```

Host 3 receives the ARP request issued by host 1 and returns the ARP reply to host 1. Host 3 then receives the ICMP echo request from host 1 and returns the echo reply to host 1, as shown in the following screenshot:

```
root@sdnhubvm:~[01:58]$ tcpdump -en -i h3-eth0
tcpdump: verbose output suppressed, use -v or -vv for full protocol decode
listening on h3-eth0, link-type EN10MB (Ethernet), capture size 65535 bytes
02:08:58.980664 00:00:00:00:00:01 > ff:ff:ff:ff:ff:ff, ethertype ARP (0x0806), length 42: Request who-has 10.0.0.3 tell 10.0.0.
1, length 28
02:08:58.980689 00:00:00:00:00:03 > 00:00:00:00:00:01, ethertype ARP (0x0806), length 42: Reply 10.0.0.3 is-at 00:00:00:00:00:0
3, length 28
02:08:58.988326 00:00:00:00:00:01 > 00:00:00:00:00:03, ethertype IPv4 (0x0800), length 98: 10.0.0.1 > 10.0.0.3: ICMP echo reque
st, id 23795, seq 1, length 64
02:08:58.988380 00:00:00:00:00:03 > 00:00:00:00:00:01, ethertype IPv4 (0x0800), length 98: 10.0.0.3 > 10.0.0.1: ICMP echo reply
, id 23795, seq 1, length 64
02:09:04.003036 00:00:00:00:00:03 > 00:00:00:00:00:01, ethertype ARP (0x0806), length 42: Request who-has 10.0.0.1 tell 10.0.0.
3, length 28
02:09:04.003329 00:00:00:00:00:01 > 00:00:00:00:00:03, ethertype ARP (0x0806), length 42: Reply 10.0.0.1 is-at 00:00:00:00:00:0
1, length 28
```

The preceding Net App of the simple switching hub describes the steps in implementing a Ryu application.

Net App 5 – simple router using Ryu controller

In the section, we would be simulating a router so that we add and delete routes or address for each switch and verify communication across them.

For this, we shall be using the following topology:

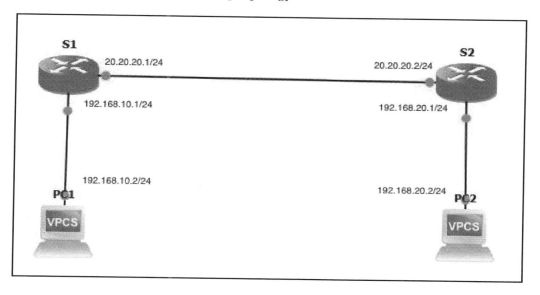

The preceding topology is a linear topology with the host, and we want the MAC to be automatically assigned. In addition to this, the scenario is implemented with the OpenFlow version 1.3 with a remote controller. Also, the rest_router.py file is going to be used for the scenario. This can be found in the ryu/ryu/app/rest_router.py directory.

Creating the topology on Mininet

We will begin this topology with the following command:

```
sudo mn --topo linear,2 --mac --switch ovsk,protocols=OpenFlow13 --
controller remote
```

```
ubuntu@sdnhubvm:~[06:32]$ sudo mn --topo linear,2 --mac --switch ovsk,protocols=OpenFlow13 --controller remote
*** Creating network
*** Adding controller
Unable to contact the remote controller at 127.0.0.1:6633
*** Adding hosts:
h1 h2
*** Adding switches:
s1 s2
*** Adding links:
(h1, s1) (h2, s2) (s2, s1)
*** Configuring hosts
h1 h2
*** Starting controller
c0
*** Starting 2 switches
s1 s2 ...
*** Starting CLI:
mininet>
```

IP address configuration on the hosts

Next, we would be editing the IP addresses of the host in accordance with the preceding topology. This can be achieved by deleting the default IP assigned to the host (10.0.0.1):

```
mininet>h1 ip addr del 10.0.0.1/8 dev h1-eth0
```

The correct IP address is then reassigned to the port of the host:

```
mininet> h1 ip addr add 192.168.10.2/24 dev h1-eth0
```

The same step shall be repeated for the other host (h2):`

```
mininet> h2 ip addr del 10.0.0.2/8 dev h2-eth0
mininet> h2 ip addr add 192.168.20.2/24 dev h2-eth0
```

Configuring the default gateway on the host

Once the hosts have been configured with the correct IP address, it is required that we configure the correct default gateway for both hosts. To achieve this, we will use the following syntax:

```
mininet> <host id> route add default gw x.x.x.x
```

For Host 1, we will have the following:

```
mininet> h1 route add default gw 192.168.10.1
```

For Host 2, we will have the following:

```
mininet> h2 route add default gw 192.168.20.1
```

To verify the preceding configuration, we can run the following command:

```
mininet> <host id> route -n
```

For host 1, run the h1 route -n command:

```
mininet> h1 route -n
Kernel IP routing table
Destination     Gateway         Genmask         Flags Metric Ref    Use Iface
0.0.0.0         192.168.10.1    0.0.0.0         UG    0      0        0 h1-eth0
192.168.10.0    0.0.0.0         255.255.255.0   U     0      0        0 h1-eth0
```

For host 2, run the h2 route -n command:

```
mininet> h2 route -n
Kernel IP routing table
Destination     Gateway         Genmask         Flags Metric Ref    Use Iface
0.0.0.0         192.168.20.1    0.0.0.0         UG    0      0        0 h2-eth0
192.168.20.0    0.0.0.0         255.255.255.0   U     0      0        0 h2-eth0
```

Starting the Ryu controller

The next step we will carry out is starting the Ryu controller using the following command:

```
>cd ryu
>bin/ryu-manager --verbose ryu/app/rest_router.py
```

```
ubuntu@sdnhubvm:~[00:50]$ cd ryu
ubuntu@sdnhubvm:~/ryu[07:05] (master)$ bin/ryu-manager --verbose ryu/app/rest_router.py
loading app ryu/app/rest_router.py
loading app ryu.controller.ofp_handler
instantiating app None of DPSet
creating context dpset
creating context wsgi
instantiating app ryu/app/rest_router.py of RestRouterAPI
instantiating app ryu.controller.ofp_handler of OFPHandler
BRICK dpset
  PROVIDES EventDP TO {'RestRouterAPI': set(['dpset'])}
  CONSUMES EventOFPSwitchFeatures
  CONSUMES EventOFPPortStatus
  CONSUMES EventOFPStateChange
BRICK RestRouterAPI
  CONSUMES EventDP
  CONSUMES EventOFPFlowStatsReply
  CONSUMES EventOFPStatsReply
  CONSUMES EventOFPPacketIn
BRICK ofp_event
  PROVIDES EventOFPPacketIn TO {'RestRouterAPI': set(['main'])}
  PROVIDES EventOFPStatsReply TO {'RestRouterAPI': set(['main'])}
  PROVIDES EventOFPPortStatus TO {'dpset': set(['main'])}
  PROVIDES EventOFPStateChange TO {'dpset': set(['main', 'dead'])}
  PROVIDES EventOFPSwitchFeatures TO {'dpset': set(['config'])}
  PROVIDES EventOFPFlowStatsReply TO {'RestRouterAPI': set(['main'])}
  CONSUMES EventOFPHello
  CONSUMES EventOFPErrorMsg
  CONSUMES EventOFPEchoRequest
  CONSUMES EventOFPEchoReply
  CONSUMES EventOFPPortDescStatsReply
  CONSUMES EventOFPSwitchFeatures
  CONSUMES EventOFPPortStatus
(24727) wsgi starting up on http://0.0.0.0:8080/
```

Upon starting the controller, it can be seen that `wsgi` is also started on `http://0.0.0.0:8080/`. This is a unified framework for connecting web applications and web servers in python. Upon execution, you should have the following log response to verify that the setup of the simple router is complete:

```
[RT][INFO] switch_id=0000000000000001: Set SW config for TTL error packet in.
[RT][INFO] switch_id=0000000000000001: Set ARP handling (packet in) flow [cookie=0x0]
[RT][INFO] switch_id=0000000000000001: Set L2 switching (normal) flow [cookie=0x0]
[RT][INFO] switch_id=0000000000000001: Set default route (drop) flow [cookie=0x0]
[RT][INFO] switch_id=0000000000000001: Start cyclic routing table update.
[RT][INFO] switch_id=0000000000000001: Join as router.
[RT][INFO] switch_id=0000000000000002: Set SW config for TTL error packet in.
[RT][INFO] switch_id=0000000000000002: Set ARP handling (packet in) flow [cookie=0x0]
[RT][INFO] switch_id=0000000000000002: Set L2 switching (normal) flow [cookie=0x0]
[RT][INFO] switch_id=0000000000000002: Set default route (drop) flow [cookie=0x0]
[RT][INFO] switch_id=0000000000000002: Start cyclic routing table update.
[RT][INFO] switch_id=0000000000000002: Join as router.
```

Configuring the address of the router (switch)

Following the preceding topology, we will be configuring the switches with the IP address using the CURL command. First, we will configure switch 1 (0000000000000001) with the address `192.168.10.1/24` and `20.20.20.1/24`:

```
</body>
root@sdnhubvm:~[07:51]$ curl -X POST -d '{"address":"192.168.10.1/24"}' http://localhost:8080/router/0000000000000001
[{"switch_id": "0000000000000001", "command_result": [{"result": "success", "details": "Add address [address_id=1]"}]}]root@sdnhubvm:~[07:54]$
root@sdnhubvm:~[07:54]$
root@sdnhubvm:~[07:56]$
root@sdnhubvm:~[07:56]$
```

```
root@sdnhubvm:~[08:36]$ curl -X POST -d '{"address":"20.20.20.1/24"}' http://localhost:8080/router/0000000000000001
[{"switch_id": "0000000000000001", "command_result": [{"result": "success", "details": "Add address [address_id=2]"}]}]root@sdnhubvm:~[08:36]$
root@sdnhubvm:~[08:36]$
```

Next, we will configure switch 2 (0000000000000002) with the address
192.168.20.1/24 and 20.20.20.2/24.

```
"Node: c0" (root)                                                    — + ⊗
root@sdnhubvm:~[07:56]$ curl -X POST -d '{"address":"192.168.20.1/24"}' http://localhost:8080/router/0000000000000002
[{"switch_id": "0000000000000002", "command_result": [{"result": "success", "details": "Add address [address_id=1]"}]}]root@sdnhubvm:~[07:58]$
root@sdnhubvm:~[07:58]$
root@sdnhubvm:~[07:58]$
root@sdnhubvm:~[07:58]$
```

```
"Node: c0" (root)
root@sdnhubvm:~[08:36]$ curl -X POST -d '{"address":"20.20.20.2/24"}' http://localhost:8080/router/0000000000000002
[{"switch_id": "0000000000000002", "command_result": [{"result": "success", "details": "Add address [address_id=2]"}]}]root@sdnhubvm:~[08:37]$
root@sdnhubvm:~[08:37]$
root@sdnhubvm:~[08:37]$
```

Note that this IP is not assigned physically to the switch but is logically saved in the
controller.

Configuring the default gateway of the switch

The next step will be configuring the default gateway on each switch. Here, the default
gateway of router 1 will be router 2 and vice versa. The following screenshot shows the
configuration of router 1. So, the default gateway here will be 20.20.20.2:

```
"Node: c0" (root)
root@sdnhubvm:~[08:40]$ curl -X POST -d '{"gateway": "20.20.20.2"}' http://localhost:8080/router/0000000000000001
[{"switch_id": "0000000000000001", "command_result": [{"result": "success", "details": "Add route [route_id=1]"}]}]root@sdnhubvm:~[08:41]$
root@sdnhubvm:~[08:41]$
```

While the following figure shows the configuration of router 2. So the default gateway here
will be 20.20.20.1:

```
"Node: c0" (root)
</html>root@sdnhubvm:~[08:39]$ curl -X POST -d '{"gateway": "20.20.20.1"}' http://localhost:8080/router/0000000000000002
[{"switch_id": "0000000000000002", "command_result": [{"result": "success", "details": "Add route [route_id=1]"}]}]root@sdnhubvm:~[08:39]$
root@sdnhubvm:~[08:40]$
root@sdnhubvm:~[08:40]$
```

Verification

Upon configuring the default gateway of both switches, the ICMP request from the host 1 (h1) is replied to from host 2 (h2):

```
mininet> h1 ping h2
PING 192.168.20.2 (192.168.20.2) 56(84) bytes of data.
From 192.168.10.2 icmp_seq=1 Destination Host Unreachable
From 192.168.10.2 icmp_seq=2 Destination Host Unreachable
From 192.168.10.2 icmp_seq=3 Destination Host Unreachable
^C
--- 192.168.20.2 ping statistics ---
5 packets transmitted, 0 received, +3 errors, 100% packet loss, time 4000ms
pipe 3
mininet> xterm c0
mininet> xterm c0
mininet> h1 ping h2
PING 192.168.20.2 (192.168.20.2) 56(84) bytes of data.
64 bytes from 192.168.20.2: icmp_seq=1 ttl=62 time=14.8 ms
64 bytes from 192.168.20.2: icmp_seq=2 ttl=62 time=0.292 ms
64 bytes from 192.168.20.2: icmp_seq=3 ttl=62 time=0.060 ms
64 bytes from 192.168.20.2: icmp_seq=4 ttl=62 time=0.062 ms
64 bytes from 192.168.20.2: icmp_seq=5 ttl=62 time=0.078 ms
^C
--- 192.168.20.2 ping statistics ---
5 packets transmitted, 5 received, 0% packet loss, time 4009ms
rtt min/avg/max/mdev = 0.060/3.076/14.891/5.908 ms
mininet>
```

Conclusion

The preceding Net App displays the functionality of the rest router existing on the RYU controller and how it can be configured.

Net App 6 – simple firewall using Ryu controller

In this section, we would be simulating a simple firewall that filters flow based on the destination IP address and the source IP address. For this, we will be using the single topology, which has three hosts, one switch, and one controller.

In this Net App, we will be utilizing the firewall application written in the Ryu controller directory. This can be found in the `ryu/ryu/app/rest_firewall.py` directory.

Creating the topology on Mininet

The topology is created using the following script:

<pre>**ubuntu@sdnhubvm:~[13:29]$ sudo mn --topo single,3 --mac --switch ovsk,protocols=OpenFlow13 --controller remote –x**

```
ubuntu@sdnhubvm:~[13:29]$ sudo mn --topo single,3 --mac --switch ovsk,protocols=OpenFlow13 --controller remote -x
*** Creating network
*** Adding controller
*** Adding hosts:
h1 h2 h3
*** Adding switches:
s1
*** Adding links:
(h1, s1) (h2, s1) (h3, s1)
*** Configuring hosts
h1 h2 h3
*** Running terms on :0.0
*** Starting controller
c0
*** Starting 1 switches
s1 ...
*** Starting CLI:
mininet>
mininet>
```

As stated earlier, this command creates a single topology with three hosts, one switch, and one controller. Also, the OpenFlow version is slated as 1.3 and the xterm to all the nodes will be opened.

Starting the rest firewall application

The next step we will carry out starts the Ryu firewall application using the following command:

```
>cd ryu
> bin/ryu-manager --verbose ryu/app/rest_firewall.py
```

```
[FW][INFO] dpid=0000000000000001: Join as firewall.
```

Once there is a successful connection between the controller and the firewall, the preceding result should be generated. The switch ID, `dpid=0000000000000001`, can be seen to be registered as a firewall.

Enabling the firewall

The firewall is not enabled by default after being initiated. To enable it, we have to run the following command on the xterm of controller `0`:

```
# curl -X PUT http://localhost:8080/firewall/module/enable/0000000000000001
```

The status of the firewall can be checked using the following command:

```
# curl http://localhost:8080/firewall/module/status
```

Creating rules

In the following example, we will be creating rules to match the following conditions:

- Source: `10.0.0.1/32`, destination: `10.0.0.2/32`, protocol: `ICMP`, and permission: allow
- Source: `10.0.0.2/32`, destination: `10.0.0.1/32`, protocol: `ICMP`, permission: allow

It should be noted that the rule ID is assigned automatically. To implement the first rule, we will execute the following command on the xterm of the controller:

```
curl -X POST -d '{"nw_src": "10.0.0.1/32", "nw_dst": "10.0.0.2/32",
"nw_proto": "ICMP"}' http://localhost:8080/firewall/rules/0000000000000001
```

Similarly, we will implement the second rule using the following command:

```
curl -X POST -d '{"nw_src": "10.0.0.2/32", "nw_dst": "10.0.0.1/32",
"nw_proto": "ICMP"}' http://localhost:8080/firewall/rules/0000000000000001
```

Verifying that these rules have been set

The following rules, which have been set previously, need to be verified so that they are present in the controller. To achieve this, we have to log in to the controller and execute the following:

```
curl http://localhost:8080/firewall/rules/0000000000000001
```

ICMP Verification

As seen in the following screenshots, host 1 (10.0.0.1) can send and receive ICMP packets from host 2 and vice versa but not host 3 (10.0.0.3). The screenshot depicts hosts not communicating with the server:

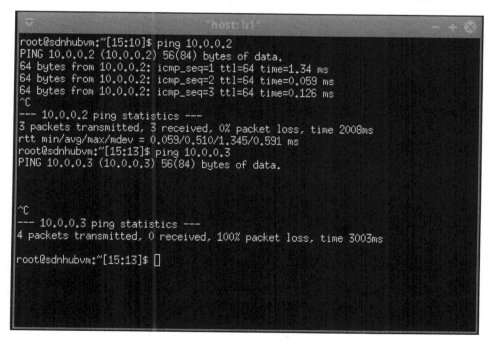

Configuring deny instructions

Inter-host communication can be stopped using the deny instruction, which is similar to the allow instruction. In order to achieve this, you need the following:

- A rule with higher priority
- A deny configuration following a similar format

```
curl -X POST -d '{"nw_src": "10.0.0.2/32", "nw_dst": "10.0.0.3/32",
"nw_proto": "ICMP", " actions": "DENY", "priority": "10"}'
http://localhost:8080/firewall/rules/0000000000000001
```

Conclusion

The preceding Net App shows how a simple white-list firewall can filter the packet flow based on the IP address of the host.

Summary

In this chapter, we presented sample network applications that utilized the OpenFlow and SDN controllers as a platform to perform networking applications. In particular, we started with a simple hub functionality over the POX controller and then we moved toward layer 2 learning switching functionality. By adding more logic to this learning switch, we demonstrated how easily we can perform packet inspection as it could be done in a simple firewall by extending the learning switch. Finally, we saw a simple packet forwarding Net App, which utilized the OpenDaylight SDN controller. In the next chapter, we will look at network virtualization and how to get a network slice.

7
Getting a Network Slice

In this chapter, network slicing with FlowVisor is discussed. The following topics will be covered:

- Network virtualization
- FlowVisor as an open source tool for OpenFlow-based network slicing
- FlowVisor API, FLOW_MATCH, and slice action structures
- Network slicing using Mininet

Network virtualization

Network virtualization is a particular abstraction of the physical networking infrastructure that provides support for multiple logical (virtual) network infrastructures (for example, set of switches, routes, and links) on top of a common physical (real) infrastructure.

The analogy of network virtualization is depicted in the following diagram:

The analogy of computer virtualization and network virtualization

On the left side of this diagram we can see a conventional computer virtualization, which is the virtual machine environment. In this environment the physical processor (CPU), memory, and input/output are abstracted by a hypervisor, on top of which a virtual machine can be run. This hypervisor essentially ensures the isolation of access to underlying resources and resource management. Similarly, a physical network can also be virtualized. On the right side of the preceding diagram, the network virtualization layer shown is responsible for providing an isolated view of the physical network infrastructure. Building a virtual network requires the technology to build virtual nodes (for example, Xen virtual machine monitor, Linux network namespaces, **Kernel-based Virtual Machine (KVM)**, VMware, and VirtualBox). There are also other possible ways to create virtual links. These are essentially based on tunneling technology.

One possibility is to get an Ethernet frame of a virtual node and encapsulate it in an IP packet that may travel through multiple hops in the network. This technique essentially provides a virtual Ethernet link using tunneling technology (for example, Ethernet **Generic Routing Encapsulation (GRE)** tunneling, **Virtual Extensible Local Area Network (VxLAN)**, and **Stateless Transport Tunneling (STT)**, among others).

There are also technologies such as Open vSwitch that provide virtual switches. It's worth mentioning that **Software-Defined Networking (SDN)** separates data plane and control plane, but the goal of network virtualization is to construct multiple virtual networks on top of a physical networking infrastructure.

FlowVisor

An SDN can have some level of logical decentralization, with multiple logical controllers. An interesting type of proxy controller, called FlowVisor, can be utilized to add a level of network virtualization to OpenFlow networks and allow multiple controllers to simultaneously control overlapping sets of physical switches. Initially developed to allow experimental research to be conducted on deployed networks alongside production traffic, it also facilitates and demonstrates the ease of deploying new services in SDN environments. FlowVisor can be considered as a special-purpose OpenFlow controller that acts as a transparent proxy between OpenFlow switches on one side and multiple OpenFlow controllers on the other side as depicted in the following diagram:

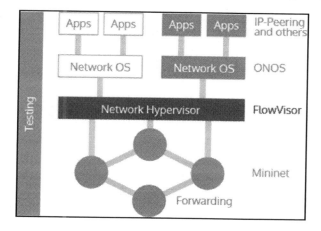

FlowVisor as a network slicer

FlowVisor creates rich *slices* of network resources and delegates control of each slice to a different controller and also promotes isolation between slices. FlowVisor, originally developed at Stanford University, has been widely used in experimental research and education networks to support slicing where multiple experimenters get their own isolated slice of the infrastructure and control it using their own network OS and a set of control and management applications.

FlowVisor enables you to conduct network research in real production environments and using real network traffic. As an open source proxy controller, you can customize the code to adapt to your needs; with a configuration and monitoring interface in **JavaScript Object Notation (JSON)** for users, and a Java programming language for developers, everyone has the ability to customize by opting to different services. You can freely and quickly experiment with SDN with all the foundational SDN functions that enable you to learn about network virtualization and test new methods for deploying services rapidly.

Since it is based on open standards that can run on a multi-vendor infrastructure, it supports multiple vendors (for example, NEC, HP, Pronto, OVS, and so on) as well as multiple guest network OSes (for example, OpenFlow controllers).

 You can find more information about FlowVisor and source code at `https://github.com/OPENNETWORKINGLAB/flowvisor/wiki?`. The instructions for installation from binary are given at `https://github.com/OPENNETWORKINGLAB/flowvisor/wiki/Installation-from-Binary`.

Isolation mechanism

Isolation achieved in the overall network is as a result of isolation of individual resources shared between each network slice. We shall be covering the various resources that are isolated and how it is being achieved.

Bandwidth isolation

Bandwidth isolation is achieved in FlowVisor by maximizing the VLAN priority code point, which is a 3-bit field in a frame ranging from 0-7 and can be used to prioritize different classes of traffic. OpenFlow protocol allows VLAN tags such as the PCP field to be managed, which makes it possible to give certain priority to packets in a flow.

Implementing bandwidth isolation involves modifying the flow table of all slices in the network as well as setting the VLAN priority field by FlowVisor. Traffic from every slice is then mapped to one of the eight priority groups, granting the network administrator capability to prioritize the bandwidth per slice.

Topology isolation

The OpenFlow protocol is used to discover the nodes and links in a given topology. In a FlowVisor virtualized environment, the FlowVisor controller acts as a proxy between the switch and the controller. Coming to the ports present on the physical switch, FlowVisor edits the OpenFlow message response to indicate only ports that are present in the virtual topology.

Neighbor discovery using the **Link Layer Discovery Protocol (LLDP)** is unique in a virtualized environment. In a **non-virtualized topology (NOX)**, the controller sends out LLDP messages from its switch ports. Once the messages are received by the switches they are sent back to the controller because they do not match any forwarding rules. With this, the neighbor database is built by NOX. FlowVisor simply intercepts the messages from the controller and tags it with the respective sending slice ID so responses are sent to the right slice once they are received again.

Switch CPU isolation

CPU utilization in a network is an essential parameter that has to be monitored very closely. This is due to the fact that an overloaded CPU will result in switches not responding to OpenFlow requests which in turn leads to LLDP timeout. These events make the controller believe there are link-flaps present in the network, leading to distorted networks.

There are four events that utilize the maximum resources of a switch CPU, and each requires unique isolation mechanisms:

- New flow messages
- Controller requests
- Slow-path packet forwarding
- Internal state keeping

New flow messages

In the OpenFlow network, the arrival of a packet that does not match any flow in the flow table leads to the generation of a new flow message toward the controller. Re-occurrence of these messages results in high CPU resource consumption.

FlowVisor manages this by setting a threshold for the new flow message arrival rate in each slice. In the event that certain packets exceed this threshold, a drop packet forwarding rule is inserted for a certain period of time.

Controller requests

A controller continuously sends certain request messages to the switches which consume CPU resources.

FlowVisor limits the CPU utilization of each slice of the controller by setting a threshold (maximum message rate per second), which allows optimum maximization of the CPU resource.

Slow-path packet forwarding

Packets in a network can either traverse a fast (hardware dedicated) forwarding path or a slow path which utilizes more CPU resources.

FlowVisor mitigates the over-utilization by limiting the number of slow-path forwarding rules injected into the network by a guest controller.

Internal state keeping

Nodes in the network utilize the CPU for keeping their internal counters, process events, and update counters updated. This in turn can have a significant effect on the performance of the switch.

FlowVisor implements a rate limit that ensures the CPU is not exhausted.

Flowspace isolation

In an environment where FlowVisor is implemented, flows in each slice of the topology must be confined to their respective flowspaces. Message rewriting is the technique used by FlowVisor to ensure that flows in one slice do not interfere with those in other slices. There are instances where the rules cannot be rewritten to suite a particular slice; such occurrences lead to the FlowVisor sending an error message to the controller that such a flow entry cannot be injected into the flowspace.

OpenFlow control isolation

The OpenFlow control channel is virtualized and isolated in the environment to ensure the efficiency in the network. Certain resources need to be virtualized by the FlowVisor for the guest controllers. For instance, a 32-bit integer is used by OpenFlow to identify the specific buffer where a packet is temporarily stored pending the forwarding decision being provided to the controller. FlowVisor must ensure that individual guest controllers access only their individual buffers.

Other messages that affect various slices such as link-down on a certain port are duplicated by FlowVisor to those respective ports.

FlowVisor API

FlowVisor is able to provide slices of network resources and convey the control of each slice to a different OpenFlow controller. Slices can be defined by any combination of packet contents from layer 1 to 4 including:

- Switch ports (layer 1)
- Source/destination Ethernet MAC address or Ethernet type (layer 2)
- Source/destination IP addresses or type (layer 3)
- Source/destination TCP/UDP port or ICMP code/type (layer 4)

FlowVisor provides and enforces slice isolation. This isolation means that the data traffic in one slice cannot be captured by hosts in another slice. The FlowVisor API is transiting from XML-RPC to JSON. The XML-RPC API will remain as is but in a deprecated state and eventually it will be removed from the API. FlowVisor users are advised to migrate any of their dependencies on the FlowVisor API to the JSON interface. The API syntax may change in some areas. Check the latest FlowVisor documentation for the updated syntax. A command-line tool can be used to access the API of FlowVisor. This tool is named `fvctl`. For example, the following command line shows how `list-slices` is invoked using the `fvctl` command-line tool:

```
$ fvctl list-slices
```

The FlowVisor API includes the following commands:

- The `list-slices` command can be used to list the currently configured slices.
- The `list-slice-info <slicename>` command shows the URL address of the control, which controls the specified `slicename`. In addition, the information of slice owner who has created the slice and his/her contact information will be shown.
- The `add-slice <slicename> <controller_url> <email>` command creates a new slice. The `slicename` cannot contain any of the following special characters: !, :, =, [,], or new lines. The format of the URL address of the controller is specified as `tcp:hostname[:port]`, for exaample `tcp:127.0.0.1:12345`. The default port (if not specified) is `6633`. The email address is used as the administrative contact point of the slice.
- The `update-slice <slicename> <key> <value>` command enables a slice user to modify the information associated with their slice. At the time of writing, only `contact_email`, `controller_host`, and `controller_port` can be changed.
- The `list-flowspace` command prints the flow-based slice policy roles, which are also called flowspaces.
- The `remove-slice <slicename>` command deletes a slice and releases all of the flowspace corresponding to the slice.
- The `update-slice-password <slicename>` command changes the password, which is associated with the `slicename` parameter.
- The `add-flowspace <NAME> <DPID> <PRIORITY> <FLOW_MATCH> <SLICEACTIONS>` command creates a new slice policy rule (flowspace) with its given `NAME`. The format of `DPID`, `FLOW_MATCH`, and `SLICEACTIONS` are explained in the following subsections.
- The `update-flowspace <NAME> <DPID> <PRIORITY> <FLOW_MATCH> <SLICEACTIONS>` command modifies the slice policy rule, which is indicated by the `NAME` parameter with a new rule with the specified parameters. The format of `DPID`, `FLOW_MATCH`, and `SLICEACTIONS` are explained in the following subsections.
- The `remove-flowspace <NAME>` command deletes the policy rule with the specified `NAME`.

FLOW_MATCH structure

How a flow matches an incoming packet is explained in the following field assignments. The FLOW_MATCH field is treated as a wildcard if any of these assignment statements is removed from the syntax of a flow. Therefore, if all of these fields are removed, then the resulting flow matches all packets; all or any can be used to specify a flow that matches all packets.

- The in_port=port_no assignment matches physical port port_no with the port number of the incoming packet. Switch ports are numbered as they are listed by fvctl getDeviceInfo DPID command.

- The dl_vlan=vlan assignment matches IEEE 802.1Q virtual LAN tag vlan with the value of the VLAN in the incoming packet. In order to match packets not tagged with a VLAN, you can specify 0xffff as the value of vlan parameter. Otherwise, specify a numeric value between 0 and 4095 (inclusive) as the 12-bit VLAN ID to match.

- The dl_src=mac assignment matches Ethernet source MAC address mac. This MAC address should be specified as six pairs of hexadecimal digits delimited by colons, like 00:0A:E4:25:6B:B0.

- The dl_dst=mac assignment matches Ethernet destination MAC address mac.

- The dl_type=ethertype assignment matches Ethernet protocol type ethertype, which should be specified as an integer between 0 and 65535 (inclusive) either in decimal or as a hexadecimal number prefixed by 0x (for instance to match ARP packets, you can specify 0x0806 as the value of ethertype).

- The nw_src=ip[/netmask] assignment matches IPv4 source address ip (specified as an IP address, for example 192.168.0.1). The optional netmask provides a mechanism to only match on the prefix of an IPv4 address. The netmask is specified in **CIDR style**; for example, something like 192.168.1.0/24.

- The nw_dst=ip[/netmask] assignment matches IPv4 destination address ip with the destination address of the incoming packet. The netmask allows the prefix matching (for instance 192.168.1.0/24).

- The nw_proto=proto assignment matches IP protocol type proto field, which should be specified as a number integer value between 0 and 255 (for instance 6 to match TCP packets).

- The `nw_tos=tos/dscp` assignment matches the ToS/DSCP field of IPv4 header value `tos/dscp` with the same quantity of the incoming packets. This value should be specified as an integer value between 0 and 255.
- The `tp_src=port` assignment matches transport-layer (for instance TCP, UDP, or ICMP) source port `port`. It should be specified as an integer number between 0 and 65535 (in the case of TCP or UDP) or between 0 and 255 (in the case of ICMP).
- The `tp_dst=port` assignment matches transport-layer destination `port`. The value should be in the same range that was mentioned for the transport layer source port.

Slice actions structure

Slice actions is a list of slices that have control over a specific flowspace. This list is comma separated and the slice actions are of the form `Slice:slicename1=perm[Slice:slicename2=perm[...]]`. Each slice possibly has three types of access permissions over a flowspace, which are 60;DELEGATE, READ, and WRITE. Permissions are currently specified as an integer bit mask value. The assignment is: DELEGATE=1, READ=2, WRITE=4. So, `Slice:alice=5,bob=2` would give DELEGATE and WRITE (1+4 = 5) permissions to Alice's slice and only read permissions to Bob.

FlowVisor slicing

In this section, you will learn how to slice your OpenFlow network, construct logical networks over a physical infrastructure, and have each slice controlled by an OpenFlow controller. You will also learn during this process the concept of flowspaces and how the centralized control feature of OpenFlow provides flexible network slicing. The network topology for this exercise is shown in the following diagram, which includes four OpenFlow switches and four hosts.

Switches **s1** and **s4** are connected to each other through **s2** via a low-bandwidth connection (that is, 1 Mbps and defined as `LBW_path` in the following custom topology script) and are also connected to each other via **s3** through a high-bandwidth (that is, 10 Mbps, defined as `HBW_path` in the custom script) set of links:

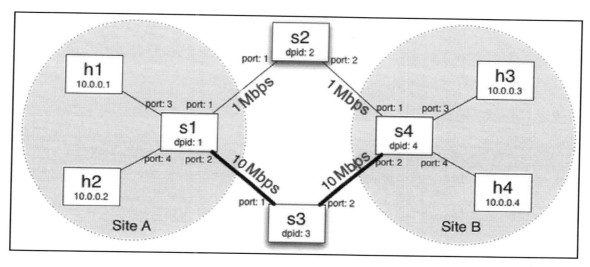

Network topology

This network topology can be constructed using the following Mininet script (assuming that the `flowvisor_topo.py` file is available in the current directory). Mininet installation was presented in Chapter 3, *Implementing the OpenFlow Switch*, utilized as part of the OpenFlow laboratory in Chapter 5, *Setting Up the Environment*:

```
$ sudo mn --custom flowvisor_topo.py --topo slicingtopo --link tc
--controller remote --mac --arp
```

The customized Python script defines a topology named `slicingtopo`, which then becomes accessible on the command line of Mininet:

```
#!/usr/bin/python
# flowvisor_topo.py
from mininet.topo import Topo
class FVTopo(Topo):
    def __init__(self):
        # Initialize topology
        Topo.__init__(self)
        # Create template host, switch, and link
        hconfig = {'inNamespace':True}
        LBW_path = {'bw': 1}
```

```
HBW_path = {'bw': 10}
host_link_config = {}
# Create switch nodes
for i in range(4):
    sconfig = {'dpid': "%016x" % (i+1)}
    self.addSwitch('s%d' % (i+1), **sconfig)
# Create host nodes (h1, h2, h3, h4)
for i in range(4):
    self.addHost('h%d' % (i+1), **hconfig)
# Add switch links according to the topology
self.addLink('s1', 's2', **LBW_path)
self.addLink('s2', 's4', **LBW_path)
self.addLink('s1', 's3', **HBW_path)
self.addLink('s3', 's4', **HBW_path)
# Add host links
self.addLink('h1', 's1', **host_link_config)
self.addLink('h2', 's1', **host_link_config)
self.addLink('h3', 's4', **host_link_config)
self.addLink('h4', 's4', **host_link_config)
topos = { 'slicingtopo': ( lambda: FVTopo() ) }
```

After the network topology, the next step is to create a configuration for FlowVisor, which will be run in a new console terminal. Assuming that you have already installed FlowVisor on a separate virtual machine, the following command line creates this configuration:

```
$ sudo -u flowvisor fvconfig generate /etc/flowvisor/config.json
```

The `fvadmin` password can be left blank by just hitting the return (*Enter*) key when prompted. To activate this configuration, simply start FlowVisor:

```
$ sudo /etc/init.d/flowvisor start
```

Using the `fvctl` utility, enable the FlowVisor topology controller. The `-f` command-line parameter points to a password file. Since no password is set for FlowVisor, the password file could point to /dev/null. In order to activate this change, FlowVisor should be restarted:

```
$ fvctl -f /dev/null set-config --enable-topo-ctrl
$ sudo /etc/init.d/flowvisor restart
```

All the OpenFlow switches in the Mininet should connect to the FlowVisor when it is started. By getting the configuration of FlowVisor, ensure that it is properly running:

```
$ fvctl -f /dev/null get-config
```

You will see the following FlowVisor configuration (in JSON format), similar to the following screen output if it is running properly:

```
{
  "enable-topo-ctrl": true ,
  "flood-perm": {
   "dpid": "all",
   "slice-name": "fvadmin"
  },
  "flow-stats-cache": 30,
  "flowmod-limit": {
   "fvadmin": {
     "00:00:00:00:00:00:00:01": -1,
     "00:00:00:00:00:00:00:02": -1,
     "00:00:00:00:00:00:00:03": -1,
     "00:00:00:00:00:00:00:04": -1,
     "any": null
   }
  },
  "stats-desc": false,
  "track-flows": false
}
```

FlowVisor configuration in JSON format

Using the following command, list the existing slices and ensure that fvadmin (the default slice) is the only one, which is shown in the output of the fvctl command:

```
$ fvctl -f /dev/null list-slices
```

Issue the following command to print the existing flow spaces and ensure that there are no existing flowspaces:

```
$ fvctl -f /dev/null list-flowspace
```

Listing the datapaths will ensure that all the switches have connected to the FlowVisor. You can check it by executing the following fvctl command. Before executing the command, you might have to wait for a few seconds. This will give enough time to the switches (**s1, s2, s3,** and **s4**) to connect to FlowVisor:

```
$ fvctl -f /dev/null list-datapaths
```

In the next step, ensure that all the network links are active by running the following command:

```
$ fvctl -f /dev/null list-links
```

The output will print out the DPIDs and source and destination ports, which are connected to each other.

Now, we are ready to slice the network. In this experiment, we will create two physical slices, which are named **Slice: Upper** and **Slice: Lower**, as shown in the following diagram:

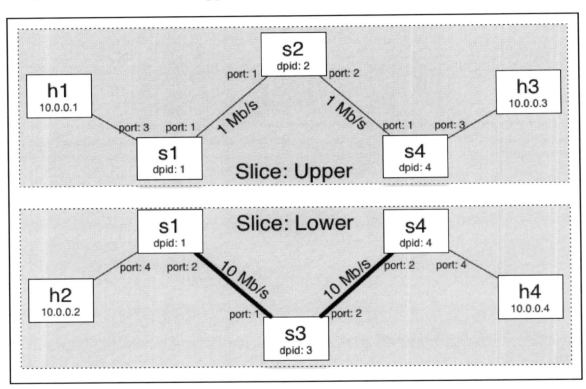

Upper and Lower slices of the experimental network

Each slice can be controlled by a separate controller, which will control all the packet traffic in its own slice. The following command creates a slice named `upper` and connects it to a controller listening on `tcp:localhost:10001`:

```
$ fvctl -f /dev/null add-slice upper tcp:localhost:10001 admin@upperslice
```

Leave the slice password empty by pressing return *(Enter)* when prompted. Similarly, you can create a slice named `lower` and connect it to a controller listening on `tcp:localhost:10002`. Again, leave the slice password empty by hitting return *(Enter)* when prompted:

```
$ fvctl -f /dev/null add-slice lower tcp:localhost:10002 admin@lowerslice
```

Now, by executing the `list-slices` command, ensure that the slices were successfully added:

```
$ fvctl -f /dev/null list-slices
```

Besides the default `fvadmin` slice, you should be able to see both the upper and lower slices, and all of them should be enabled. In the next step, you will create flowspaces. Flowspaces associate packets of a particular type to specific slices. When a packet matches more than one flowspace, FlowVisor assigns it to the flowspace with the highest priority number. The description of flowspaces comprises a series of comma-separated `field=value` assignments. You can learn more about the `add-flowspace` command like this:

```
$ fvctl add-flowspace -h
```

Now, we create a flowspace named `dpid1-port1` (with priority value 1) that maps all the traffic on port 1 of switch **s1** to the upper slice in the network topology. This can be done by executing the following command:

```
$ fvctl -f /dev/null add-flowspace dpid1-port1 1 1 in_port=1 upper=7
```

Here we give the upper slice all permissions: DELEGATE, READ, and WRITE (1 + 4 + 2 = 7). In a similar way, we create a flowspace named `dpid1-port3` that maps all the traffic on port 3 of switch **s1** to the upper slice in the network:

```
$ fvctl -f /dev/null add-flowspace dpid1-port3 1 1 in_port=3 upper=7
```

By using the match value of `any`, we can create a flowspace for matching all the traffic at a switch. So, we add switch **s2** to the upper slice by running the following command:

```
$ fvctl -f /dev/null add-flowspace dpid2 2 1 any upper=7
```

Now, we create two more flowspaces (`dpid4-port1` and `dpid4-port3`) to add ports 1 and 3 of switch **s4** to the upper slice:

```
$ fvctl -f /dev/null add-flowspace dpid4-port1 4 1 in_port=1 upper=7
$ fvctl -f /dev/null add-flowspace dpid4-port3 4 1 in_port=3 upper=7
```

Ensure that these flowspaces are correctly added by running the following command:

```
$ fvctl -f /dev/null list-flowspace
```

You should see all the flowspaces (five in total) that you just created. Now, we create flowspaces for the lower slice:

```
$ fvctl -f /dev/null add-flowspace dpid1-port2 1 1 in_port=2 lower=7
$ fvctl -f /dev/null add-flowspace dpid1-port4 1 1 in_port=4 lower=7
$ fvctl -f /dev/null add-flowspace dpid3 3 1 any lower=7
$ fvctl -f /dev/null add-flowspace dpid4-port2 4 1 in_port=2 lower=7
$ fvctl -f /dev/null add-flowspace dpid4-port4 4 1 in_port=4 lower=7
```

Again, ensure that the flowspaces are correctly added:

```
$ fvctl -f /dev/null list-flowspace
```

Now you can launch two OpenFlow controllers on your local host, which are listening on ports `10001` and `10002`, corresponding to the upper and lower slices. You should also write a small Net App that reactively installs routes based on the destination MAC address. After a short delay, both controllers should connect to FlowVisor. Now, you can verify that host h1 can ping h3 but not h2 and h4 (and vice versa).

Run the following command in the Mininet console:

```
mininet> h1 ping -c1 h3
mininet> h1 ping -c1 -W1 h2
mininet> h1 ping -c1 -W1 h4
```

Verify that h2 can ping h4 but not h1 and h3 (and vice versa). Run the following command in the Mininet console:

```
mininet> h2 ping -c1 h4
mininet> h2 ping -c1 -W1 h1
mininet> h2 ping -c1 -W1 h3
```

This concludes a simple network slicing using switch ports. However, by defining other slicing rules and developing other Net Apps, you can provide interesting and innovative services for each slice. For instance, you can differentiate traffic and treat them accordingly across the upper and lower network slices. We leave this to you as an exercise.

FlowVisor is a great controller with certain limitations considering the fact that certain resources cannot be virtualized. Virtual links in the FlowVisor topology are dependent on the physical infrastructure currently existing. Creating a complex virtual topology will require future modifications in the FlowVisor controller.

Flowspace maximization is also another limitation in FlowVisor. For instance, a certain IP address block 20.0.0.0/16 might want to be used by two slices; with FlowVisor it is impossible to maximize it simultaneously.

Summary

In this chapter, we introduced the concept of network virtualization and, in particular, the role and functionality of FlowVisor as a tool for network slicing in OpenFlow-based networks. The FlowVisor API and related structures for flow matching and slice actions were presented and a use case experiment was explained in this chapter. Now you are aware of the tools that can be used to slice a network and control each slice in an innovative way.

In the next chapter, we will look at the roles of OpenFlow and SDN in general in cloud computing.

8
OpenFlow in Cloud Computing

This chapter focuses on the role of OpenFlow in cloud computing and in particular the installation and configuration of Neutron. One of the promises of **Software-Defined Networking (SDN)** and OpenFlow is the improvement that they can introduce in data centers and cloud computing infrastructure. Therefore, it is worth covering the usage of OpenFlow (for instance, the Floodlight plugin for OpenStack) in data centers and in particular OpenStack as one of the widely used control and management software for cloud computing.

A brief introduction of OpenStack and its networking component (which is called Neutron as of writing this) and its overall architecture will be discussed in this chapter. In particular, the installation and configuration of the Floodlight OpenFlow controller plugin will be explained. Interested readers are recommended to consider this chapter as a pointer to further details that can be found in the documentation of OpenStack Networking.

We will discuss the following topics:

- OpenStack and Neutron
- OpenStack Networking architecture
- Neutron plugins

OpenStack and Neutron

OpenStack is a cloud computing system software (sometimes referred to as cloud computing OS), that delivers **Infrastructure as a Service (IaaS)**. Released under the Apache license, OpenStack is free open source software. The OpenStack Foundation was established in September 2012 as a non-profit corporate entity that manages the OpenStack project. It promotes OpenStack and its developer community. OpenStack includes a set of building-block projects that control pools of computing nodes (that is, processing nodes), storage, and networking resources in a data center. OpenStack provides a dashboard that enables administrators to control and provision these resources through a web-based (GUI) interface. OpenStack's modular architecture and its building blocks (and their code names) are shown in the following diagram:

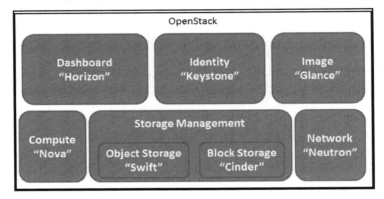

Key components of OpenStack

OpenStack Compute (nova), which is the main part of an IaaS system, is the cloud computing fabric controller. Nova is written in Python and it utilizes many external libraries such as SQLAlchemy (for database access), Kombu (for **Advanced Message Queuing Protocol (AMQP)** communication), and Eventlet (for concurrent programming). Nova is able to manage and automate pools of computer resources and can cooperate with widely available virtualization technologies and **high-performance computing (HPC)** deployments.

It is designed to scale horizontally on commodity computers with no proprietary hardware or software requirements and also to provide the ability to integrate with third-party technologies and legacy systems. Xen server and **Kernel Virtual Machine (KVM)** are the typical choices for hypervisor technology, along with Linux container technology such as **Linux containers (LXC)** and Hyper-V.

OpenStack utilizes two components for its storage management:

- **Swift**: It is used for object storage management. Swift is also known as OpenStack Object Storage. It is a redundant and scalable storage system. Files and objects are written to multiple disks across multiple servers in the data center. The OpenStack software is responsible for ensuring data integrity and replication across the cluster. By adding new servers, storage clusters simply scale horizontally. If a server or hard drive fails, OpenStack replicates its content to new locations in the cluster from other active nodes. Since OpenStack uses software algorithms to ensure data distribution and data replication across different devices, inexpensive commodity hard disks and servers can be used for storage management.

  Storage by Swift makes scaling much less buggy as more focus needs to be placed on the best approach to ensure data is backed up in the event of a crisis against capacity supported by a single system.

  Swift is currently being led by an object storage software company, SwiftStack, though contribution is also received from HP, Red Rat, IBM, and more. SwiftStack is currently working on a project called ProxyFS that will add distributed file services to OpenStack Swift. This will enable the support of the **Server Message Block (SMB)** and **Network File System (NFS)** protocols.

- **Cinder**: It provides persistent block-level storage devices for use with OpenStack Compute instances. It uses a SQL-based central database that is utilized by all Cinder services in the system. Cinder is also known as OpenStack Block Storage. The block storage system is responsible for managing the creation, attachment, and detachment of the block devices on the servers. Block storage is suitable for performance-sensitive scenarios such as expandable filesystems and database storage or for providing a server with access to raw block-level storage devices. Block storage volumes are fully integrated into nova (OpenStack Compute) and OpenStack's dashboard.

  This enables cloud users to easily manage their own storage requirements. Powerful functionality for backing up data stored on block storage volumes is provided by snapshot management. Snapshots can be used to create a new block storage volume or simply can be restored. It comprises various components:

  - **DB**: A SQL database for data storage that is used by all components
  - **Web dashboard**: This is an external component that communicates with the API

- **API**: This is the component responsible for receiving HTTP requests, interpreting them to commands, and communicating with other components via the queue or HTTP
- **Auth manager**: This is a Python class utilized for the users/projects and roles by most components
- **Scheduler**: This allocates the volume that is assigned to each host
- **Volume**: This manages the block devices attached dynamically
- **Backup**: This is responsible for managing backup of block storage devices

Horizon is the OpenStack dashboard. It provides a GUI for users and administrators to provide, automate, and access cloud-based resources. It consists of three dashboards: user, system, and settings . Third-party products and services, such as monitoring, billing, and additional management tools, can be integrated into Horizon (OpenStack dashboard).

Using the native OpenStack API or the Amazon EC2 compatibility API, developers can automate, access, or build customized tools to manage their resources. OpenStack APIs are compatible with Amazon S3 and Amazon EC2. Therefore, client applications designed and developed for **Amazon Web Services (AWS)** can be used with OpenStack.

Keystone (the OpenStack Identity component) provides a central directory of users, which are mapped to their accessible OpenStack services. It functions as a common authentication system across the cloud operating system. It can also be integrated with existing backend directory services such as LDAP. Standard username and password credentials, token-based systems, and AWS logins are the many authentication mechanisms that are supported by Keystone.

Currently, it supports authN, which is token-based and user-service authorization. Support for proxying external services and authN/authZ mechanisms such as oAuth, SAML, and OpenID have been introduced in view of the future.

Keystone comprises major components listed as follows:

- **User**: These are basically digital representations of a person, system, or service that utilizes OpenStack cloud services.
- **Tenant**: This can be referred to as a group utilized for the isolation of resources and/or users. It is usually allocated to organizational units, projects, and customers.

- **Role**: This describes a group of certain user rights and privileges that have been assigned for undertaking certain operations. The *user token* issued by Keystone comprises all the user's roles.
- **Credentials**: This is a set of data, usually a username and password, username and API key, or authentication token that is known to a specific user to prove his or her identity.
- **Authentication**: This involves validating the credentials that were earlier supplied by the user.
- **Token**: This is an arbitrary bit of text to access resources across the platform. It is usually valid for a limited time span.
- **Service**: OpenStack services provided to one or more endpoints, allowing users to access resources and perform operations.
- **Endpoint**: A network-accessible address from which services are rendered, usually presented by a URL.

Glance (OpenStack Image service) provides discovery, registration, and delivery services for server images and disks. Stored server images can be used as a template. It can be also used to store and catalog an infinite number of backups. Glance can store disk and server images in a variety of backends, including Swift. A standard **Representational State Transfer (REST)** interface is provided by Glance for querying information about disk images and enables clients to stream the disk images to new servers.

Glance, when integrated with existing infrastructure, enhances their performance. Integration with VMware enables advanced performance such as VMotion, the live migration of **virtual machines (VMs)** from one physical server to another, high availability, and dynamic resource scheduling (DRS).

Neutron (formerly known as Quantum) is the networking component of OpenStack. It manages networks and IP addresses. Starting with the Folsom release, Neutron is a supported and core part of the OpenStack platform. Like other component of the cloud operating system, administrators and users can utilize Neutron to increase the utilization of existing resources in a data center. Neutron provides **Networking as a Service (NaaS)** between interface devices (for instance vNICs), which are managed by other OpenStack services.

OpenStack Neutron provides networking models for different user groups or applications. Standard models include VLANs or flat networks for separation of network traffic among different servers. Neutron also manages IP addresses, which can provide dedicated static IPs or DHCP-based IP addressing. Floating IP addressing allows packet traffic to be dynamically rerouted to any of the computing nodes, which facilitates traffic redirection during VM migration, maintenance, or failure handling.

The extensible architecture of Neutron paves the way for additional network services, such as firewalls, **intrusion detection systems (IDS)**, VPN, and load balancing to be deployed and managed. The networking component of OpenStack provides OpenStack's users with an API to construct rich networking topologies and configure advanced network policies to construct a multi-tier web application topology.

The modular structure of Neutron facilitates the development of innovative plugins, which introduce advanced network capabilities (such as L2-in-L3 tunneling to bypass the VLAN 4k limitation, end-to-end **Quality of Service (QoS)** guarantees, and utilization of monitoring protocols such as NetFlow and OpenFlow plugins). Besides, developers can develop advanced network services that integrate into the OpenStack tenant network using plugins. For instance, data-center-interconnect-aaS, IDS-aaS, firewall-aaS, VPN-aaS, and load-balancing-aaS are a few typical advanced services to mention. Using Neutron, users can create their own networks, control traffic, and connect servers and devices to one or more networks, while administrators can take advantage of SDN technology (for instance OpenFlow) to provide high levels of multi-tenancy and scalability.

Nova is the brain of the IaaS; it manages and automates the pool of resources. Nova also integrates with bare metal (using ironic), virtualization technologies, and HPC. Nova is based in Python and also utilizes extra external libraries including `Eventlet`, `Kombu`, and `SQLAlchemy`. Nova is dependent on Keystone, Glance, and Neutron for optimum performance.

Ceilometer is a data collection service that facilitates the normalization and transformation of data across all the OpenStack core components. Its primary targets are monitoring and metering, but the framework is expandable to collect usage for other needs.

OpenStack Networking architecture

Neutron is able to utilize a set of backends called plugins that support a growing set of networking technologies. These plugins may be distributed separately or as part of the main Neutron release. OpenStack Networking (Neutron) is a virtual network service that provides an efficient API to define the network connectivity and addressing, which is used by devices from other OpenStack services (such as OpenStack Compute). The OpenStack Networking API utilizes virtual network, subnet, and port abstractions to describe networking resources. In the OpenStack networking ecosystem:

- A network is an isolated L2 segment similar to VLAN in physical networking.
- A block of IPv4 or IPv6 addresses and associated configuration states is a subnet.

- A connection point for attaching a single device, such as the NIC of a virtual server, to a virtual network is defined as a port. Also, a port describes the network configuration parameters (such as the MAC and IP addresses) associated with that port.

By creating and configuring networks and subnets, users can configure rich network topologies and then instruct other OpenStack services such as OpenStack Compute to connect virtual interfaces to ports on these networks. Neutron particularly supports each tenant having multiple private networks, and enables tenants to choose their own IP addressing scheme. The OpenStack Networking service:

- Provides advanced cloud networking scenarios, such as constructing multi-tiered web applications and enabling applications to be migrated to the cloud without IP address modifications.
- Enables cloud administrators to offer flexible and customized network offerings.
- Provides API extensions that lets cloud administrators expose additional API capabilities. These new capabilities are typically introduced as an API extension, and gradually will become part of the core OpenStack Networking API.

The original OpenStack Compute network implements a very simple model of traffic isolation through IP tables and Linux VLANs. OpenStack Networking introduces the notion of a plugin, which is a backend implementation of the OpenStack Networking API. A plugin can use different technologies to implement logical API requests. Some OpenStack Networking plugins might use basic Linux VLANs and IP tables, while others might use more advanced technologies, such as L2-in-L3 tunneling or OpenFlow, to provide similar capabilities.

The main module of the OpenStack Networking server is `neutron-server`, which is a Python daemon that exposes the OpenStack Networking API. It passes user requests to the configured OpenStack Networking plugin for extra processing. The plugin typically needs a database for persistent storage. If your deployment uses a controller host to run centralized OpenStack Compute components, you can deploy the OpenStack Networking server on that same host. However, OpenStack Networking is completely standalone and can be deployed on its own server. Based on deployment, OpenStack Networking also includes additional agents that might be required, which are as follows:

- A plugin agent (`neutron-*-agent`), which executes on each hypervisor to configure the local switch. Since some plugins do not actually require an agent, the agent to be run will depend on the selected plugin.
- A DHCP agent (`neutron-dhcp-agent`) provides DHCP services to tenant networks.

- An L3 agent (`neutron-l3-agent`) provides L3/NAT forwarding to facilitate external network access for VMs on tenant networks.

These agents interact with the core Neutron process through **remote procedure call (RPC)** or by utilizing the standard OpenStack Networking API. OpenStack Networking relies on Keystone for the authentication and authorization of all API requests. Nova interacts with OpenStack Networking through standard API calls. During the VM creation process, nova communicates with the OpenStack Networking API to plug each virtual network interface card on the VM into a particular network. Horizon integrates with the OpenStack Networking API, and enables tenant users and administrators to create and manage network services through the GUI of the OpenStack dashboard.

There are four distinct physical data center networks in a standard OpenStack Networking deployment, as depicted in the following diagram:

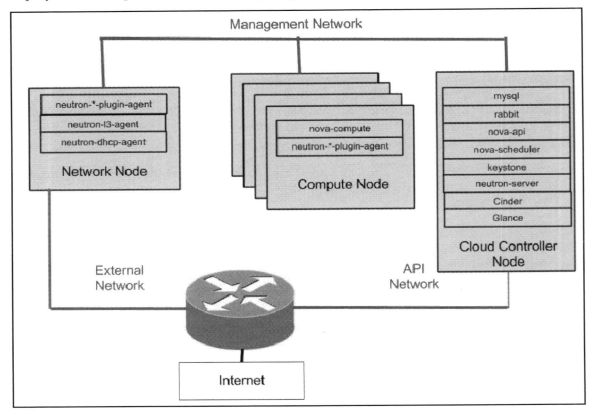

Network connectivity for physical hosts

- **Management network**: It is used for internal communication between OpenStack components. IP address assignments on this network should be only reachable within the data center network.

- **Data network**: It is used for VM data communication within the cloud setup. Depending on the networking plugin used, the IP addressing requirements of this network vary.

- **External network**: It is used to provide internet access for VMs in some deployments. IP addresses on this network should be visible and reachable by any host on the internet.

- **API network**: It exposes all OpenStack APIs, including the OpenStack Networking API, to tenants. IP addresses on this network should be reachable by anyone on the internet.

 The complete installation and configuration instructions of OpenStack Neutron can be found in the OpenStack networking administration guide. More information can be found here: `https://wiki.openstack.org/wiki/Neutron`.

Neutron plugins

Providing rich cloud networking by enhancing traditional networking solutions is quite challenging. Traditional networking is not scalable to cloud proportions by its design nor able to cope with automatic configuration. OpenStack Networking introduces the concept of a plugin, which is a backend implementation of the OpenStack Networking API. In order to implement logical API requests, a plugin can utilize a variety of technologies. Some plugins might use Linux IP tables and basic VLANs, while other implementations might use more advanced technologies, such as L2-in-L3 tunneling or OpenFlow.

Plugins can have different features for hardware requirements, properties, performance, scale, or operator tools. OpenStack supports a wide spectrum of plugins. Therefore, the cloud administrator is able to consider different options and decide which networking technology fits a particular use case scenario. Among different plugins for Neutron, in this section, we will consider the Floodlight controller plugin for OpenStack Neutron.

Utilizing a Neutron plugin, Floodlight can be run as the network backend for OpenStack. Neutron exposes a NaaS model via a REST API, which is implemented by Floodlight. This solution includes two main components: the Neutron RestProxy plugin that connects Floodlight to Neutron and a VirtualNetworkFilter module in Floodlight that implements the Neutron API. The VirtualNetworkFilter module implements MAC-based layer 2 network isolation in OpenFlow networks and exposes it through a REST API.

This module is included in Floodlight by default and does not depend on Neutron or OpenStack to be active and running. The VirtualNetworkFilter can be activated through a configuration file change described later in the chapter. The RestProxy plugin was designed to run as part of OpenStack's Neutron service. Floodlight with the Big Switch Neutron plugin supports the OpenStack Grizzly release.

The Floodlight OpenStack support is enabled by:

- The Big Switch Neutron plugin at the OpenStack Neutron main repository, `https://github.com/openstack/neutron`
- The OpenStack `devstack` repository `stable/grizzly` branch at `https://github.com/ist0ne/OpenStack-Grizzly-Install-Guide-CN`

The following instructions are for setting up Floodlight and OpenStack (Grizzly) on an Ubuntu VM using `devstack` scripts developed by Big Switch. A virtual machine with Ubuntu Server 12.04.1 or a later version is required. The outcome of this procedure is a single-node OpenStack installation with Floodlight as its Neutron backend. Tenants, virtual networks, and virtual instances can be created by the OpenStack Horizon GUI (dashboard).

You will need to execute a Floodlight controller for the OpenStack Neutron networking support to properly function. The floodlight controller can be running on a separate Floodlight VM or you can obtain and download the Floodlight source as a compressed ZIP file, unzip it, compile it, and run it with the following simple steps on your Ubuntu VM. Make sure you have internet connectivity before proceeding.

```
$ sudo apt-get update
$ sudo apt-get install zip default-jdk ant
$ wget --no-check-certificate
https://github.com/floodlight/floodlight/archive/master.zip
$ unzip master.zip
$ cd floodlight-master; ant
$ java -jar target/floodlight.jar -cf src/main/resources/neutron.properties
```

To confirm the VirtualNetworkFilter is successfully activated, enter the following commands on your Ubuntu VM:

```
$ curl 127.0.0.1:8080/networkService/v1.1
{"status":"ok"}
```

Once Floodlight is confirmed running, we are ready to install OpenStack using the `install -devstack` script. The following are the steps:

1. It configures the OVS switch on the VM to listen to the Floodlight controller.
2. Then it installs OpenStack and the Big Switch REST proxy plugin on the VM.
3. If you want the OpenStack Grizzly release, use the following commands:

```
$ wget https://github.com/openstack-
dev/devstack/archive/stable/grizzly.zip
$ unzip grizzly.zip
$ cd devstack-stable-grizzly
```

4. If you want the OpenStack Folsom release, use the following commands:

```
$ wget
https://github.com/bigswitch/devstack/archive/floodlight/
folsom.zip
$ unzip folsom.zip
$ cd devstack-floodlight-folsom
```

5. Use your favorite editor to create a file named `localrc` and fill in the following details. Remember to replace <password> with your chosen password and update `BS_FL_CONTROLLERS_PORT=<floodlight IP address>` with the value `8080`. If you have run Floodlight in the same VM, then use `127.0.0.1` for `<floodlight IP address>`; otherwise, use the IP address of the VM or host where Floodlight is running:

```
disable_service n-net
enable_service q-svc
enable_service q-dhcp
enable_service neutron
enable_service bigswitch_floodlight
Q_PLUGIN=bigswitch_floodlight
Q_USE_NAMESPACE=False
NOVA_USE_NEUTRON_API=v2
SCHEDULER=nova.scheduler.simple.SimpleScheduler
MYSQL_PASSWORD=<password>
RABBIT_PASSWORD=<password>
ADMIN_PASSWORD=<password>
SERVICE_PASSWORD=<password>
SERVICE_TOKEN=tokentoken
DEST=/opt/stack
SCREEN_LOGDIR=$DEST/logs/screen
SYSLOG=True
#IP:Port for the BSN controller
#if more than one, separate with commas
```

```
BS_FL_CONTROLLERS_PORT=<ip_address:port>
BS_FL_CONTROLLER_TIMEOUT=10
```

6. Then enter the following command:

```
$ ./stack.sh
```

Note that OpenStack installation is a long process that cannot be interrupted. Any interruption or loss of network connectivity results in unknown states that cannot be resumed. It is recommended that you take a snapshot using VirtualBox before you begin the installation so that you can easily power down and restore the original snapshot if indeed the process is interrupted.

The script `install-devstack.sh` requires uninterrupted IP connectivity to run. If the installation completes successfully, it will show the following screen:

```
Horizon is now available at http://10.10.2.15  /
Keystone is serving at http://10.10.2.15:5000/v2.0/
Examples on using novaclient command line is in
exercise.sh
The default users are: admin and demo
The password: nova
This is your host ip: 10.10.2.15
stack.sh completed in 103 seconds.
```

You can verify the installation of OpenStack and Floodlight using the instructions in the following link: `https://floodlight.atlassian.net/ wiki/spaces/floodlightcontroller/pages/1343607/ Install+Floodlight+and+OpenStack+on+Your+Own+Ubuntu+VM.`

Summary

Neutron is an OpenStack project to provide NaaS among interface devices (known as virtual NICs) managed by other OpenStack services (nova). Starting with the Folsom release of OpenStack, Neutron is a core and supported part of the OpenStack framework. In this chapter, the key building blocks of OpenStack, including the Neutron networking component and the backend plugins (specifically the Floodlight plugin), were introduced. The Neutron API includes support for L2 networking and **IP Address Management (IPAM)**. An API Extensibility platform, including extensions for the provider network, which maps Neutron L2 networks to a specific VLAN in the physical data center and the network L3 routers supports a simple L3 router construct to route between L2 networks. It also provides a gateway to external networks with support for floating IP addresses.

In the next chapter, we'll look at a selection of key open source projects around SDN and OpenFlow.

9
Open Source Resources

Software-Defined Networking (SDN) and OpenFlow are among the hot topics in the networking research and development domain both in industry and academia. There are plenty of active open source projects around the SDN and OpenFlow that form OpenFlow software-based switches to OpenFlow controllers, orchestration tools, network virtualization tools, simulation and testing tools, and so on. The main idea here is to give a brief and condensed summary of active open source projects around SDN and OpenFlow. We will cover the following open source projects:

- **Controllers**: Beacon, Floodlight, Maestro, Trema, FlowER, Ryu, **Open Network Operating System (ONOS)**, Atrium, and OpenContrail
- **Miscellaneous**: FlowVisor, FlowSim, Avior, RouteFlow, OFlops and Cbench, OSCARS, Twister, FortNOX, Nettle, Frenetic, and OESS.

This chapter gives pointers to the important projects that network engineers can utilize in their operational environment.

Controllers

In Chapter 5, *Setting Up the Environment*, we covered POX, OpenDaylight, and Floodlight OpenFlow controllers. In this section, we provide a list of other open source OpenFlow controller alternatives.

Beacon

Beacon is a fast, cross-platform, modular, Java-based controller that supports both event-based and threaded operations. It has been in development since early 2010 and has been used in several research projects, networking classes, and trial deployments. It is written in Java and runs on many platforms, from high-end multi-core Linux servers to Android phones. Beacon is licensed under a combination of the GPL v2 license and the Stanford University FOSS License Exception v1.0. Code bundles in Beacon can be started/stopped/refreshed/installed at runtime without interrupting other non-dependent bundles. For example, you can replace your running `Learning Switch` Net App without disconnecting switches.

The API present in Beacon is simple so that developers can utilize any available Java constructs, ranging from timers to sockets. OpenFlowJ is an object-oriented Java implementation of the OpenFlow 1.0 specification. The `OpenFlowJ` library present in Beacon is used when communicating with OpenFlow messages. It contains codes that serialize and write message objects to the wire and deserialize messages coming off the wire into objects. The `IBeaconProvider` interface is used for interacting with OpenFlow switches.

The interface `IOFSwitchListener` is the method used to register listeners that are notified when switches are added and removed from the topology. The interface `IOFInitializerListener` is the method used to perform switch initialization and the interface `IOFMessageListener` is the method used for receiving specific OpenFlow messages types.

There are certain reference applications that build on the core used for adding additional APIs, which are as follows:

- **Device Manager**: This is used to track any device present in the network. It tracks parameters such as their MAC addresses, IP addresses, the last seen date, the switch last present on, and the port of the switch. It also provides the `IDeviceManato` interface to search for known devices also to register to receive events when new devices are added, updated, or removed.

- **Topology**: This is used to discover the links between connected OpenFlow switches. It comprises an interface (`ITopology`) that enables the retrieval of a list of such links and event registration to be notified when links are added or removed.

- **Routing**: This is used to provide the shortest path layer two routing between devices in the network. This application exports the `IRoutingEngine` interface, allowing interchangeable routing engine implementations. Routing here is highly dependent on both topology and device manager.

- **Web**: This provides a web UI for Beacon. The web application provides the `IWebManageable` interface, enabling implementers of the interface to add their own UI elements.

 You can find more information about this controller at `https://openflow. stanford.edu/display/Beacon/Home`.

Floodlight

The Floodlight Open SDN Controller is an enterprise-class, Apache-licensed, Java-based OpenFlow Controller. It is supported by a community of developers, including a number of engineers from Big Switch Networks. Floodlight is written in Java and thus runs within a JVM. The source code repository is available on GitHub. The easiest way to get started with Floodlight is to download the Floodlight VM appliance.

In addition to it being an OpenFlow controller, Floodlight is also a collection of applications built on top of the Floodlight Controller. The controller realizes a set of common functionalities to control and inquire an OpenFlow network, while applications on top of the Floodlight controller realize different features to solve different user requirements over the network. The architecture of Floodlight is shown in the following diagram.

The relationship among the Floodlight Controller, the applications built as Java modules compiled with Floodlight, and the network applications built over the Floodlight REST API are shown in the following diagram:

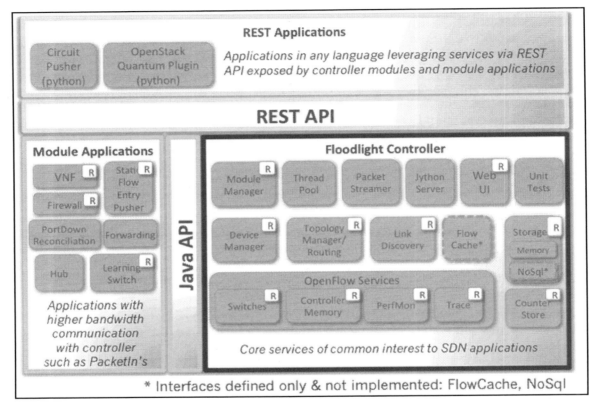

Architecture of the Floodlight controller and Net Apps

When you start the Floodlight controller, a set of Java module applications, which are loaded in the Floodlight properties file (for example, learning switch, hub, firewall, and static flow entry pusher) start running too. The REST APIs exposed by all running modules are available via the specified REST port (8080 by default). Other Net Apps (for example, the OpenStack quantum plug-in or circuit pusher) can utilize this REST API to retrieve information and invoke services by sending HTTP REST commands to the controller REST port.

You can find more information about Floodlight at `http://www.projectfloodlight.org/floodlight/`.

Maestro

Maestro is a network operating system for orchestrating network control applications. It provides interfaces for implementing modular network control applications to access and modify the state of the network and coordinate their interactions via multiple protocols, including OpenFlow. Although it can be considered an OpenFlow controller, Maestro is not limited to OpenFlow networks. The programming framework of Maestro provides interfaces for the following:

- Introducing new customized control functions by adding modularized control components
- Maintaining the network state on behalf of the control components
- Composing control components by specifying the execution sequencing and the shared network state of the components

Maestro is developed on Java (both the platform and the components), which makes it highly portable to various operating systems and architectures. It also takes full advantage of multi-core processors using multithreading techniques. Maestro is licensed under the GNU Lesser General Public License version 2.1.

 For more details about downloading, using, and programming Maestro, visit `https://code.google.com/archive/p/maestro-platform/`.

Trema

Trema is an OpenFlow controller framework that includes everything needed to create OpenFlow controllers in Ruby and C. The Trema source package includes basic libraries and functional modules that work as an interface to OpenFlow switches. Several sample applications developed on top of Trema are also provided, so you can run them as a sample of OpenFlow controllers.

Additionally, a simple but powerful framework that emulates an OpenFlow-based network and end hosts is provided for testing your own controllers. A Wireshark plug-in to diagnose internal data flows among functional modules is provided as a debugging tool. Currently, Trema supports GNU/Linux only and has been tested on the following platforms:

- Ubuntu 13.04, 12.10, 12.04, 11.10, and 10.04 (i386/amd64, desktop edition)
- Debian GNU/Linux 7.0 and 6.0 (i386/amd64)
- Fedora 16 (i386/x86_64)
- Ruby 1.8.7
- RubyGems 1.3.6 or higher

It may also run on other GNU/Linux distributions but is not tested and not supported at the time of writing this.

 You can find more information about Trema at `https://github.com/trema`.

FlowER

FlowER is an open source Erlang-based OpenFlow controller. Its purpose is to provide a simplified platform for writing network control software in Erlang. It is currently under development, but Travelping (`http://www.travelping.com/`), the creator of FlowER, is already using it in its commercial products. FlowER is built for a deployment model that packages each Erlang application either as an RPM or DEB package.

 You can find more information about FlowER at `https://github.com/travelping/flower`.

Ryu

Ryu is a component-based SDN framework that integrates with OpenStack and supports OpenFlow. It provides a logically centralized controller and well-defined API that make it easy for operators to create new network management and control applications. Ryu provides software components with a well-defined API that makes it easy for developers to create new network management and control applications. Ryu supports various protocols for managing network devices, such as OpenFlow (1.0, 1.2, 1.3 and Nicira extensions), **Network Configuration Protocol** (**NETCONF**), OF-Config, and so on. The goal of Ryu is to develop an operating system for SDN that has quality high enough for use in a large production environment. All of the code is freely available under the Apache 2.0 license. Ryu is developed openly.

Utilizing Ryu, operators can create tens of thousands of isolated virtual networks without using VLAN. You can create and manage virtual networks, which will be propagated to OpenStack and the Ryu plugin. Ryu, in turn, configures Open vSwitches properly. A preconfigured Ryu VM image file enables the operators to easily set up a multinode OpenStack environment. Ryu is implemented in Python, and its development is truly open.

 You can find more information about Ryu at `http://osrg.github.io/ryu/`.

Open Network Operating System

Open Network Operating System, which represents **ONOS**, provides the control plane for a SDN, managing network components, such as switches and links, and running software programs or modules to provide communication services to end hosts and neighboring networks. It is the first open source network OS designed for service providers and mission-critical networks. Its aim is to provide high availability and optimum performance to these networks.

In server operating systems, ONOS provides analogous functionalities, some of which are APIs and abstractions, resource allocation, and permissions, as well as user-facing software such as a CLI, a GUI, and system applications. ONOS is used to manage the entire network rather than a single device in traditional switching operating systems, which, in turn. simplifies the management, configuration, and deployment of new software, hardware, and services. In SDN controllers, ONOS acts as an extensible, modular, and distributed SDN controller for the whole network.

ONOS kernel, core services, and ONOS applications are written in Java as bundles that are loaded into the karaf OSGi container. OSGi is a component system for Java that allows modules to be installed and run dynamically in a single JVM. Since ONOS runs in the JVM, it can run on several underlying OS platforms.

ONOS comprises four major features that make the architecture. They are as follows:

- **Distributed core**: This provides the service provider features (scalability and high availability) to the control plane of SDN. The same ONOS software is generally deployed on the cluster of servers present on the network. As a result of this, the network applications and network devices do not know whether they are working on a single instance or multiple instances of ONOS, thus providing network scalability for the network administrator. The distributed core is the main architectural feature that presents the service-provider-grade features to the SDN control plane.
- **Northbound abstraction/API**: This includes the network graph and applications whose purpose is to ease the development of control, management, and configuration services. It comprises two abstractions, that is, internet framework and global network view:
    - The internet framework permits an application to request a certain service from the network without prior knowledge of how the service will be performed. Network administrators and application developers use this to their advantage in high-level network programming. A common example of intent would be setting up an optical path between switch A and switch B and restricting the bandwidth assigned to the path.
    - The global network view is used to give the application a view of the network. This view gives the application the capability to program the network via the API. Each API allows the application look at the view as a network graph. Network graphs can be used in traffic engineering, practically by maximizing the network utilization by monitoring the network view and programming changes to the path to adjust the load.

- **Southbound abstraction/API**: The southbound is a key component for migration from traditional switches to open flow white boxes. It insulates the core of ONOS from the details of diverse protocols and devices by representing each network element as an object in a generic form. This abstraction permits the distributed core to maintain the state of the network node without knowing the specifics of the element being represented. The benefits of the southbound include the ability to manage various devices using multiple protocols with no effect on the distributed core, adding new devices to the system easily, as well as a smooth migration of traditional devices and protocols to white boxes that support full OpenFlow standards.
- **Software modularity**: This is what accommodates the easy development, debugging, and maintaining of ONOS as a software system by the community of users and developers. ONOS is an open source project backed by an expanding community of developers and users.

For more information, visit `https://github.com/opennetworkinglab/onos`.

Atrium

The Atrium project was created to solve two major challenges in the development of a dynamic ecosystem. The first challenge is the rift existing between the elements required to build a hybrid SDN stack. In various layers of the stack, there are missing pieces that lead to a low integration. The second challenge lies in the fact that there is a gap in interoperability.

These challenges are found in inter-vendor interoperability and at the protocol level with interfaces being under-specified or over-specified. For instance, a connection between a switch and a controller can be affected by the number of versions of OpenFlow currently defined and the complexity of deciding what to use.

Atrium solves both challenges by instantiating and integrating a set of production quality components. ONOS is a key component in the initial distribution of Atrium. It has released the second ONOS-based Atrium route in 2016. Its architecture can be found as follows:

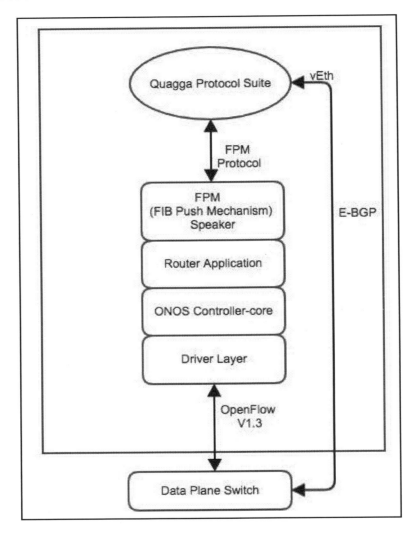

 For more information, visit `https://github.com/onfsdn/atrium-odl`.

OpenContrail

This is an extensible system for SDN, that can be used for multiple networking use cases. It comprises two major drivers in the architecture, which are as follows:

Cloud Computing:

These are primarily private clouds designed for enterprises and service providers, **Infrastructure as a Service (IaaS)**, cloud service providers, and virtual private clouds. These cases involve multi-tenant virtualized data centers where the physical resources (servers, storage boxes, and physical network) are being utilized by all tenants. The physical resources are logically (via virtual machines, virtual storage, and virtual networks) assigned to each individual tenant. The virtualized resources are siloed from one another, except that security policies are created to allow inter-tenant communication or via physical IP VPN or layer two VPN connections.

Network Function Virtualization (NFV) in service providers network:

Value added services are key components in service providers edge networks. Some major service provider edge networks include business edge networks, broadband subscriber management edge networks, and mobile edge networks. This involves the orchestration and management of functions in virtual machines, such as firewalls, deep packet inspection, and WAN optimization.

Components that make up the OpenContrail system are controller and vRouter. The OpenContrail controller is the centralized logical distributed SDN controller that is responsible for providing management, control, and analytics functions of the virtualized network. OpenContrail vRouter is basically the forwarding plane of the distributed router running in the hypervisor of a virtualized server. The physical switches and routers are extended into the virtual overlay network by the vRouter. OpenContrail vRouter can be likened to the open source switches that are available, such as the Open vSwitch, but it has more advanced functionalities such as routing and higher-level switching, from which it derived the name vRouter.

The architecture of OpenContrail can be found in the following diagram:

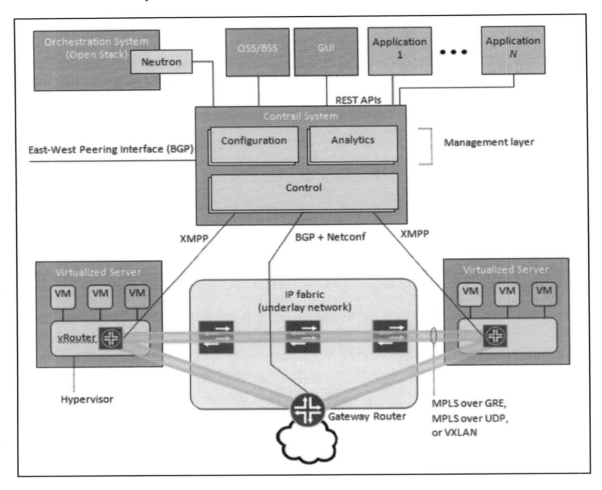

The preceding architecture comprises various components. These are as follows:

- Northbound REST APIs are primarily utilized by applications. They are used when integrating the OpenContrail with cloud orchestration systems. They are also used by other operators that provide BSS/OSS. They are also utilized to implement web-based GUI.
- Southbound interfaces are used to communicate with the virtualized vRouters and the physical routers and switches.

- East-west interfaces are used to bond with other controllers. The standard BGP present is for the east-west interface, and XMPP is used for the vRouters by the southbound interface. The gateway routers and switches utilize the BGP and NETCONF.

Miscellaneous

In addition to the soft switches and controllers, there are many other open source projects around OpenFlow and SDN. In this section, we provide pointers to some important open source projects.

FlowVisor

A SDN can have some level of logical decentralization, with multiple logical controllers. An interesting type of proxy controller, called FlowVisor, can be utilized to add a level of network virtualization to OpenFlow networks and allow multiple controllers to simultaneously control overlapping sets of physical switches. Initially developed to allow experimental research to be conducted on deployed networks alongside production traffic, it also facilitates and demonstrates the ease of deploying new services in SDN environments. FlowVisor is a special purpose OpenFlow controller that acts as a transparent proxy between OpenFlow switches and multiple OpenFlow controllers, as shown in the following figure:

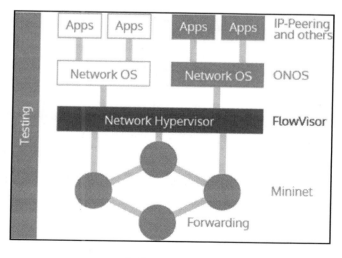

FlowVisor as a network slicer

FlowVisor creates rich slices of network resources and delegates control of each slice to a different controller and promotes isolation between slices. FlowVisor, originally developed at Stanford University, was widely used in experimental research and education networks to support slicing where multiple experimenters get their own isolated slice of the infrastructure and control it using their own network OS and a set of control and management applications.

FlowVisor enables you to conduct network research in real production environments and using real network traffic. As an open source proxy controller, you can customize the code to adapt to your needs, with a configuration and monitoring interface in JSON for users and a Java programming language for developers. Everyone has the ability to customize by opting into different services. You can freely and quickly experiment with SDN, with all the foundational SDN functions that enable you to learn about network virtualization and test new methods for deploying services rapidly. Since it is based on open standards that can run on a multi-vendor infrastructure, it supports multiple vendors (for example, NEC, HP, Pronto, OVS, and so on) as well as multiple guest network OSes (that is, OpenFlow controllers).

We introduced FlowVisor in `Chapter 6`, *How to get a Network Slice*, as part of our discussion on network virtualization; you can find more information about FlowVisor and download it at `https://github.com/OPENNETWORKINGLAB/flowvisor/wiki`.

Flowsim

Flowsim is a self-contained web application that is used to create a switch profile based on a specific version of OpenFlow. It can simulate five different instances of the OpenFlow switch data plane simultaneously. During simulation with Flowsim, internal data structures are visible, so a user can see exactly how the OpenFlow pipeline operates.

Flowsim can be used to visualize the OpenFlow pipeline and all the internal packet processing as well as to let users see the packet flow as a result of different configuration applied to the network.

With Flowsim, you can set various parameters that can be used in the simulation. They include the following:

- **Datapath**: This is used to specify the fragmentation behavior of the pipeline. Also, the number of packets that can be buffered for the controller is specified.
- **Port**: Port configuration of the switch is done here. Configurations done here include the number of ports present on the switch, the types of virtual ports, MAC address of each port, speed, and also medium (that is, fiber or copper).
- **Action**: Contents of a packet can be modified by setting certain parameters to understand how immediate packet modifications affects multi-table matching. Parameters that can be modified include forwarding it to a specific port and using a unique egress handling group.
- **Meter**: This is used to define a policy to meter a flow. It can also be used to limit flows to a certain target or allow burst outside the allowed queue depth.
- **Flow table**: This is used to specify the flow tables' capabilities such as the number of flows, matching types, and which instructions are enabled and disabled by a table.
- **Match**: This is used to test the matching of various versions of OpenFlow and multiple modeled vendor switches.
- **Group**: This is used to define a certain set of egress packet processing behaviors across multiple destinations.
- **Flow**: This is used to manipulate packets through flow configuration. You can achieve track flow statistics and manage flow life cycle explicit exclusion, inactivity timeouts, and absolute timeouts of packets.
- **Instruction**: This can be used to learn immediate and delayed packet modification and forwarding. It is also used to explore OpenFlow's control flow using goto's, partition matching across tables with metadata, and meter flow rates using policers and shapers.
- **Queue**: This is used to enable port-based queuing during profile creation. It can be utilized to understand OpenFlow's limitations about queue management and use queues as targets in output actions.

You can find more information about Flowsim at
`https://flowsim.flowgrammable.org` and
`https://github.com/flowgrammable/flowsim/blob/master/README.md`.

Avior

Avior is an application built outside of Floodlight that gives network administrators a graphical user interface to support their needs. It eliminates dependency on using Python scripts or viewing the REST API in order to monitor or manipulate the network. Avior provides an overview of a controller, switch, and device, and it includes a flow manager. The controller overview provides information about the controller, including the hostname, the JVM memory bloat, whether the controller is providing JSON data, and currently loaded modules. The switch overview provides information about ports and their associated traffic counters and flow table entries. Both dynamic and static flows are displayed with the priority, match, action, packets, bytes, duration, and timeout details. The device overview displays information about the MAC address, the IP address, the attached switch DPID, the attached switch port, and the time it was last seen in the network. The flow manager provides an overview and detailed information of the static flows for each switch. Here, you can also manage (add or delete) flow entries. In summary, Avior supports a number of useful features, as follows:

- Static flow entry pusher interface: add, modify, and delete flows easily
- Useful error checking and flow verification
- Detailed controller, switch, device, port, and flow statistics that update in real time
- Easy to use logical patch panel

 Avior is developed for the Marist OpenFlow Research project (`http://openflow.marist.edu/`). You can download it and find more information at `https://github.com/Sovietaced/Avior`.

RouteFlow

RouteFlow is an open source project to provide virtualized IP routing over OpenFlow capable hardware. It is composed of an OpenFlow controller application, an independent server, and a virtual network environment that reproduces the connectivity of a physical infrastructure and runs IP routing engines. The routing engines generate the **Forwarding Information Base** (**FIB**) in the Linux IP tables according to the routing protocols configured (for example, OSPF and BGP). RouteFlow combines the flexibility of open source Linux-based routing stacks (for example, Quagga and XORP) with the line-rate performance of OpenFlow devices.

RouteFlow allows a migration path to SDN via controller-centric hybrid IP networking, in addition to deployable innovation around IP routing and the different flavors of network virtualization. The main components of the RouteFlow solution are as follows:

- **RouteFlow Client (RF-Client)**
- **RouteFlow Server**
- **RouteFlow Proxy (RF-Proxy)**

RF-Proxy was formerly known as the **RF-Controller (RF-C)** application (refer to the following diagram). The main goal of RouteFlow is to develop an open source framework for virtual IP routing solutions over commodity hardware, which implements the OpenFlow API. RouteFlow aims at a commodity routing architecture that combines the line-rate performance of commercial hardware with the flexibility of open source routing stacks (remotely) running on general purpose computers. Migration path from legacy IP deployments to purely SDN/OpenFlow networks, open source framework to support the different flavors of network virtualization (for example, logical routers, router aggregation/multiplexing), IP Routing-as-a-Service models of networking and simplified intra and inter-domain routing interoperable with legacy networking devices are the key outcomes of design space of RouteFlow routing solutions:

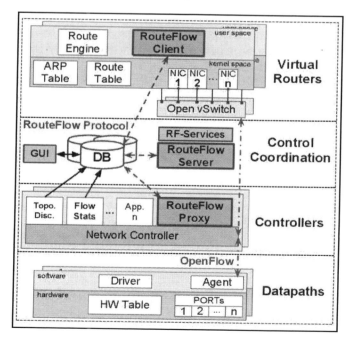

Building blocks of RouteFlow in an architectural view

You can find more information about RouteFlow at `https://sites.google.com/site/routeflow/home`.

OFlops and Cbench

OFlops is a standalone controller that benchmarks various aspects of an OpenFlow switch. OFlops implements a modular framework for adding and running implementation-agnostic tests to quantify a switch's performance. OFlops sets up a single control channel with the switch and uses multiple network ports to generate traffic on the data plane (OpenFlow switch). Besides, OFlops supports the SNMP protocol in order to read various MIB counters, such as CPU utilization, packet counters, and so on. OFlops has two building blocks:

- The executable program, which implements the core functionality of the platform
- A set of dynamically loaded libraries that implement the required functionality for a specific performance evaluation

These components communicate with each other using a rich set of event-driven APIs. Each dynamic test can implement a subset of the provided event handler and adjust the behavior of OFlops. OFlops performs multi-level high-precision measurements in order to benchmark the performance of the switch. It utilizes multi-threading parallelism. Cbench is a program for testing OpenFlow controllers by generating packet-in events for new flows. Cbench emulates a bunch of switches, which connect to a controller, send packet-in messages, and wait for flow-mods to get pushed down.

You can find more information about OFlops and Cbench at `https://github.com/mininet/oflops/tree/master/cbench`.

OSCARS

Energy Science Network (ESnet) On-Demand Secure Circuits and Advance Reservation System (OSCARS) provides multi-domain, high-bandwidth virtual circuits that guarantee end-to-end network data transfer performance. The OSCARS software works as both a framework for research innovation and as a reliable production-level service for ESnet users. While ESnet offers a menu of service components to novice users, ESnet explores an integrated services framework to assist experienced users in configuring highly modular atomic services as desired and for network researchers to customize according to experimental parameters.

 You can find more information at `https://www.es.net/engineering-services/oscars/`.

Twister

Luxoft Twister is a test automation framework designed to manage and drive test cases written in shell scripting languages. Twister supports TCL, Python, and Perl. Twister offers an intuitive, web-based user interface for the configuration, control, and reporting with remote access availability. This makes it easy to build the testing suite, execute it, and accurately monitor the result logs.

 For more information, refer to `https://github.com/Luxoft/Twister`.

FortNOX

FortNOX is an extension to the open source NOX OpenFlow controller. It automatically checks whether the new flow rules violate security policies. FortNOX can detect rule contradictions even in the presence of dynamic flow tunneling using set action rules.

 For more information, refer to `http://www.openflowsec.org/Technologies.html`.

Nettle

Nettle allows networks of OpenFlow switches to be controlled using a high-level, declarative, and expressive language. It is implemented on a Haskell library that supports the OpenFlow protocol and provides an OpenFlow server.

 You can find more information about Nettle at `http://haskell.cs.yale.edu/other-projects/nettle/`.

Frenetic

Frenetic is a domain-specific sublanguage for programming the data plane packet processing in OpenFlow networks. It presents certain unique features, such as the following:

- **High-level abstraction**: This gives the network administrator or programmer complete control over specifying how they require the network to perform with less concern about implementing it.
- **Modularity**: This presents modular constructs that support compositional reasoning about programs.
- **Portability**: This enables programs to be executed on a diverse platform.
- **Accurate foundations**: Frenetic's foundation documents the meaning of the language, which presents a great platform for analysis tools. In Frenetic, there are two major languages actively under development that handle low-level packet-processing as well as manage the traffic in the data plane when possible. These are as follows:
    - Frenetic-OCaml: This is embedded and implemented in OCaml. It is developed and supported by Cornell.
    - Pyretic: This is embedded and implemented in Python. It is developed and supported by Princeton.

 For more information, go to `https://github.com/frenetic-lang/`.

Open Exchange Software Suite

Network Development and Deployment Initiative (NDDI) Open Exchange Software Suite (OESS) is an application to configure and control OpenFlow enabled switches through a very simple and user-friendly user interface. OESS provides subsecond circuit provisioning, automatic failover, per-interface permissions, and automatic per-VLAN statistics. Though it supports multiple features, it is yet to support MAC address learning, VLAN dot1q tunneling (Q in Q), and **Quality of Service (QoS)**.

It is supported by these switches: Brocade MLXe, Cisco ASR9000, Dell S4810, IBM G8264, Juniper MX960, and NEC PF5820.

 For more information, refer to https://github.com/globalnoc/oess.

Summary

SDN and OpenFlow are among the hot topics both in academia and industry. There are a lot of commercial and open source developments around OpenFlow and SDN in general. In this chapter, we tried to provide an overview of important open source projects around SDN/OpenFlow. Beacon, Floodlight, Maestro, Trema, FlowER, and Ryu were additional SDN/OpenFlow controllers that we covered in this chapter. Besides, we also briefly mentioned other important active projects, such as FlowVisor, Avior, RouteFlow, OFLops and Cbench, OSCARS, Twister, FortNOX, Nettle, Frenetic, and OESS.

10
The Future of SDN

Programmable networks have paved the way for new methods to design, build, and operate our networks. They create a structure that supports our complex data applications such as Big Data, **Internet of Things (IoT)**, 4k video, and virtualization.

SDN's adoption into the production network is overwhelming, with major service providers such as AT&T swapping traditional network equipment for off-the-shelf servers that can run network software applications. By 2020, AT&T is expected to have 75% of its network based on SDN models considering the benefits, such as reduced capital expenditure and operation expenditure, minimized space and hardware requirement, and improved security.

We will cover the following topics:

- Packet forwarding innovations beyond OpenFlow
- Protocol-independent forwarding
- Optical transport protocol extensions
- Security extensions
- Wireless transport SDN

Packet forwarding innovations beyond OpenFlow

There are two major approaches that are in view for packet forwarding beyond OpenFlow:

- **Protocol Oblivious Forwarding (POF)**
- Programming protocol-independent packet processors (P4)

POF

This is a recent technology proposed by Huawei Technologies that supports a protocol-independent data plane in SDN. In POF, the data-plane forwarding element does not require prior knowledge of the header structure of the protocol packet it is to traverse; rather, it can be configured by the control plane with the offsets in the configuration phase.

At runtime, the offsets are extracted by the **Forwarding Elements** (FE) and lookup from the flow table is done, followed by execution of the vital instructions.

This allows the forwarding element to support new protocols easily with no need to modify its hardware as well as wired protocols, such as between controller and switch.

POF is completely unaware of the protocols running on the data plane, such as the IP, TCP, and Ethernet protocols; rather, when a packet is received, the header is extracted layer by layer and every layer consists of multiple flow tables. These flow tables also parse the header for the next layer after processing its own layer.

POF architecture

POF consists of two major components in its architecture: the POF switch and POF controller (POFOX). Protocol and metadata can be configured via the user interface through a UI. Applications create flow tables as services require. During this procedure, the protocol database could be referenced and the applications download all flow table entries into the designated device through the OpenFlow channel.

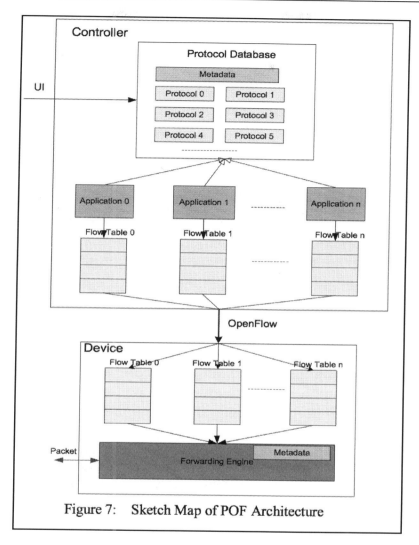

Figure 7:   Sketch Map of POF Architecture

POF controller

This is a cross-platform OpenFlow controller that is Java based and also based on OpenFlow protocol version 1.3. POF is supported on it, therefore allowing users to create new packet types and forwarding processes. POFOX functions both on physical and virtual switches that support POF. In addition to these features, it also provides a Java GUI platform that allows users to create, view, and modify the new packet types, tables, entries, and forwarding processes easily.

Structure of POFOX

POFOX consists of multiple components: the **Communication Engine, Topology Discovery**, and the spanning tree protocol component.

The **Communication Engine**, the main component, is responsible for communicating with POF-supported switches. This forms the base on which other components operate. The following diagram depicts the structure:

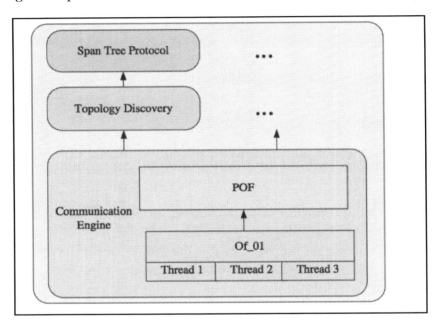

In the POF architecture, forwarding of packets is controlled strictly by the POFOX, which makes communication with the switch a high priority for POFOX.

Messages sent back and forth include the connection-establishing messages, query messages, and switch status change messages. The structure of these messages is defined and sockets are created to listen to these messages from the switch. Unpacking and forwarding of these messages is done by POFOX when it receives them, and packing of data is done when sending messages to the switch.

Topology Discovery involves building a full connection between POFOX and the POF switch using the **Link Layer Discovery Protocol (LLDP)**. Here, the switch sets up a TCP connection with POFOX and sends the HELLO message, which is replied to by POFOX. The FEATURE message is then sent to POFOX, giving it information about the features supported by the switch, as well as the PORT message, which tell POFOX about the status of the ports on the switch.

In the event where a loop exists in the topology based on the PORT messages, a spanning tree network is created where the ports that are absent from the tree are disabled.

The major drawback of POFOX is flow tables can be configured manually for the forwarding elements but programming models are not supported.

POFSwitch

This is a Linux C-based, BSD-licensed OpenFlow software switch. It is also based on the OpenFlow 1.3 protocol, similar to POFOX. It supports POF so that packets with new types can be forwarded by new user-defined forwarding processes.

POFSwitch works with POFController, which supports POF and also provides a Linux C-based platform to receive, forward, process, and send packets with the new types. The flow tables, flow entries, and forwarding processes can be created, modified, and deleted by the POFController easily.

Packet forwarding in the POFSwitch is unique because it handles packets whose destination MAC address is equal to that of the POFSwitch network port.

Programming protocol-independent packet processors

OpenFlow version one (v1.0), launched in December 2009, and was a groundbreaking innovation, with 12 header fields. Since then, reactive evolution has occurred in the various OpenFlow versions available, which has culminated in the fifth version (v1.5) released in December 2014, with more than 41 fields. The flexibility of the added header fields have been limited but complexity of the specification increased. Infrastructures such as data centers that will be implementing SDN in full scale require much more flexibility, which the present specification cannot support optimally. P4 is a high-level language that works in conjunction with OpenFlow to increase the level of abstraction in a programmed network.

P4 components

P4 comprises five major components that support such a high level of abstraction:

- **Headers**: This defines the sequence and structure of a series of fields. It includes the specification of field names, widths, and constraints on field values.
- **Parsers**: This defines how headers and valid header sequences within packets are identified.
- **Tables**: This is where the header fields are matched to the actions for packet processing. The P4 program defines the fields on which a table may match and the actions it may execute.
- **Actions**: P4 supports the construction of complex actions from simpler protocol-independent primitives. These complex actions are available within match and action tables.
- **Control programs**: This determines the order in which match action tables are applied to a packet. A simple imperative program describes the flow of control between match action tables.

Forwarding model of P4

The forwarding model comprises two operations:

- **Configure**: Here the parser is programmed and the order of the match action stages are set; also, the header fields to be processed at each stage are defined. The protocols that are supported are determined here and so is the method of packet processing.
- **Populate**: This operation adds and removes entries in the match action tables that were defined earlier. It determines the policy applied to packets at any given time.

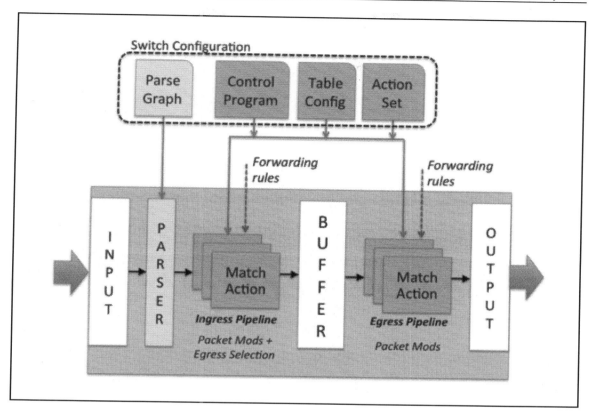

Protocol-independent forwarding

Research has been ongoing on how a common, consistent, and vendor-independent way consistent with OpenFlow can be defined to ensure packet processing by a flexible switch. The **Open Networking Foundation (ONF)** proposed the (OF-PI) approach, which was created to express new and existing protocols in the data path.

OF-PI is composed of a set of instructions that are protocol neutral, called the POF-FIS, and the P4 language, which is utilized to express the method in which forwarding of packets should be done by the forwarding plane. P4 and POF-FIS express the supported functionalities in an OpenFlow specification which is revealed as a library module existing on OF-PI. P4/POF modules could be used to express various protocols such as **Generic Routing Encapsulation (GRE)** and **Multiprotocol Label Switching (MPLS)**.

Here, P4 is used to define the formats of the packet and table structure, and POF-FIS, which is protocol independent, is used to perform actions that are specific to protocols. A diagrammatic representation of the **Proposed Protocol-independent Layer** of OF-PI is as follows:

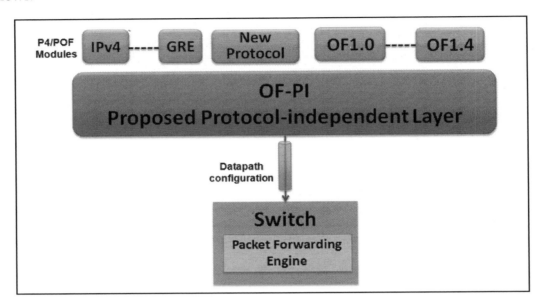

Table Type Patterns

Table Type Patterns (TTP) was developed by the ONF **Forwarding Abstraction Working Group (FAWG)** to solve the limitation of OpenFlow with respect to TCAM capabilities.

Older versions of OpenFlow (1.0, 1.1, and 1.2) were handicapped as they were not allowed to access the memory resource on the ASIC for simple forwarding applications such as routing since they utilized a single-table implementation that involved using the TCAMs for flows.

TTP utilizes the memory resources (VLAN, MAC, and IP tables) present on the ASIC to achieve this by distributing flows to suitable resources. This enhancement allowed the software layer to translate provisioned flows into single or multiple flow entries in the hardware. The ASIC architecture is required to be conformed in a TTP environment, enabling maximum scalability of SDN applications.

Relationship between TTP and OF-PI

TTP is used to represent the capabilities of a predefined data path to the controller in a bottom-to-top approach, while P4/POF is used to define the behavior of the switch's data path, which can be compiled to a loadable form to alter the data path of a programmable switch in a top-to-bottom approach.

Data path configuration is represented by both languages but from diverse perspectives. It should be noted that at runtime, a controller should not detect any difference between a fixed-function platform conforming to a specific TTP and a programmable platform configured by a P4 program to provide the same behavior.

The following diagram represents the difference between TTP and OF-PI:

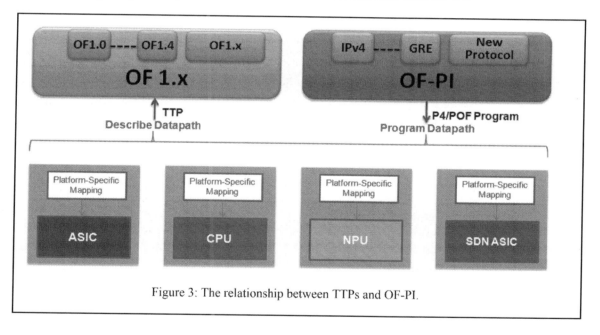

Figure 3: The relationship between TTPs and OF-PI.

Goals of OF-PI

The following are the goals of OF-PI:

- **Reconfigurable**: OF-PI was designed so that the flexible switches can be programmed to reconfigure packet parsing and processing.
- **Protocol independent**: The packet format should not conform to OpenFlow, but the network programmer should have the ability to specify a packet parser for extracting header fields with particular names and types. A collection of type-match and action tables that process these headers can be specified.
- **Target-independent**: A network programmer should not require prior knowledge of the switch architecture, but the compiler should have the capability to turn a target-independent description of how packets are to be processed into a target-dependent program (used to configure the switch).

Optical transport protocol extensions

Optical transport networks can be supported by OpenFlow in an ONF **Optical Transport Working Group** (**OTWG**) architecture. OpenFlow in data centers supports layer 2 to layer 4 networks, but support for multilayer layer 0 to layer 4 networks where OpenFlow acts as the unified interface is possible with OpenFlow covering the circuit (layer 0 and layer 4) network.

In traditional multilayer networks, every packet and optical network has its administrator, database, and **network management system** (**NMS**). In such networks, design and operation are implemented on the network individually. Changes in such a network require a long chain of discussion that can last up to weeks between the administrators to achieve this. Future operation of multilayer networks that implement an SDN/OpenFlow architecture have the resources (packet and optical) abstracted to be processes in the unified database.

Implementation of such a model has multiple advantages, such as rapid service creation, where resources needed by the optical network can be allocated in a shorter period when required by the packet network, and capital expenditure and operation expenditure costs are reduced drastically. The following diagrams give a pictorial explanation of a unified database versus the current multilayer networks:

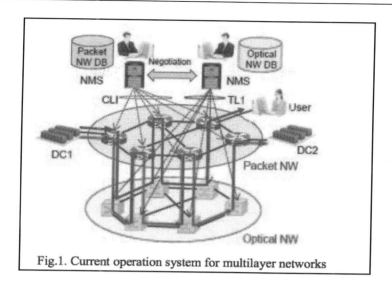

Fig.1. Current operation system for multilayer networks

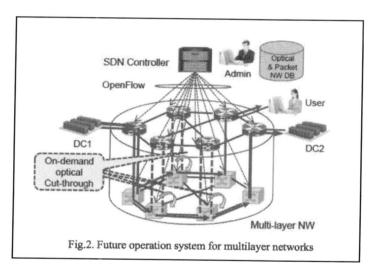

Fig.2. Future operation system for multilayer networks

Generalized Multiprotocol Label Switching

Generalized Multiprotocol Label Switching (GMPLS), also known as Multiprotocol Lambda Switching, is a technology that enhances **Multiprotocol Label Switching (MPLS)** to support more advanced network switching for time, wavelength, and space switching as well as for packet switching.

In the GMPLS scenario, every network element has a control plane, known as the C-plane, and the data plane, known as the D-plane. The optical path here is set to exchange protocol messages between various adjacent network elements. The control plane possesses a protocol controller, which is in charge of the following:

- RSVP-TE, which is a signaling protocol that reserves resources, such as for IP unicast and multicast flows, and requests **Quality of Service (QoS)** parameters for applications
- **Open Shortest Path First Traffic Engineering (OSPF-TE)** which is used to send out LSAs that have special extensions for traffic engineering
- LMP, which is used for neighbor discovery and link/resource discovery

The database in the GMPLS is used for storing the path/link details and policies.

The GMPLS suite was modified to operate with Synchronous Optical Networks, synchronous digital hierarchy, optical transport network, and wavelength division multiplexing.

Packet-optical Integration

Packet-optical Integration (POI) of networks has been implemented in various ways. O3 Orchestrator Suite, which is the framework that manages virtual resources in the multilayer network and reports changes to resources to the OpenFlow controller, has been used as the framework in most deployments.

There exist two implementations, which are **Optical Core Network Resource Manager (OCNRM)** and the OpenFlow agent implementation:

- **OCNRM**: In the OCNRM implementation, the layer 0 and layer 1 resources of the optical networks are virtualized and then registered with the ODENOS. These resources get managed by the OCNRM in collaboration with the ODENOS. Division is made in the network into two virtual network resources, the **Lower Order (LO)** unit and the **Higher Upper (HO)** unit. The LO is mapped to the client signal and the HO is mapped to the LO. The LO ODU corresponds to the ODU layer (L1), and the HO ODU to the optical channel layer (L0). The architecture of this setup is diagrammatically represented as follows:

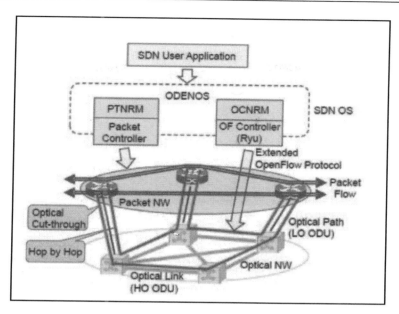

- **OpenFlow agent**: In this implementation, OpenFlow messages are translated into information used by existing optical **network elements (NEs)**. The OpenFlow agent is responsible for the translation: it translates OpenFlow messages into optical **Transaction Language 1 (TL1)** commands, which are used to control the OTN nodes with OpenFlow. The architecture of this setup is diagrammatically represented as follows:

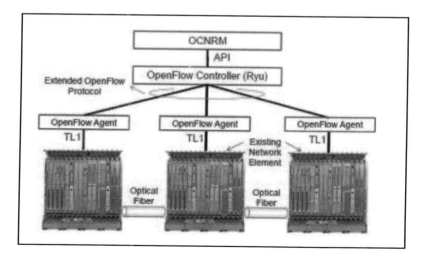

Summary

In this chapter, we discussed the various advancements that have been proposed to be added to the SDN model for improvement in performance. Also, we looked at how SDN can be integrated with optical networks and the methods with which it has been implemented.

Index

4

4D project
  URL 18

A

Access control list (ACL) 90
ad-hoc 37
Advanced Message Queuing Protocol (AMQP)
  176
Amazon Web Services (AWS) 178
Application Programming Interface (API) 76
application specific ICs (ASICs) 39
asynchronous messages, OpenFlow reference
    switch
  Flow-Removed 43
  packet-in 43
  Port-Status 44
asynchronous messages
  controller-status 36
  flow-removal 35
  packet-in 34
  port-status 35
  request-forward 36
  role-status 35
  table-status 36
Atrium
  about 197, 198
  URL 198
Avior
  about 204
  references 204

B

Beacon 190
building blocks, SDN deployment
  actions 22

  cookies 27
  counters 21
  flags 28
  header field 19
  priority 25
  timeouts 27
built-in functions
  URL 80

C

campus networks applications 12
Cbench 206
Ceilometer 180
characteristics, SDN
  central control 10
  network automation 10
  plane decoupling 8
  simple forwarding elements 10
  virtualization 10
Cloud Computing 199
command-line interface (CLI) 45
Communication Engine 214
controller-to-switch
  asynchronous configuration, setting 33
  configuration 30
  features 29
  modify-state 30
  packet-out 32
  read-state 31
  role-request 32
controllers
  about 189
  Atrium 197, 198
  beacon 190
  Device Manager 190
  Floodlight 191
  FlowER 194

Maestro 193
Open Network Operating System 195
OpenContrail 199
routing 191
Ryu 195
topology 191
Trema 193
URL 191
web 191

D

data center applications 11

E

Energy Services Network (ESnet) 207
Ethane
    URL 18
Ethernet learning switch
    about 122
    building 126

F

firewall
    about 129
    application, beginning 152
    conclusion 156
    deny instructions, configuring 156
    enabling 153
    ICMP Verification 154
    rules, creating 153
    rules, verifying 154
    simulating, with Ryu controller 151
    topology, creating on Mininet 152
first in first out (FIFO) 95
FloodLight OpenFlowHub
    URL 91
Floodlight
    about 88, 191, 192
    Firewall module 90
    network plugin, for OpenStack 91
    static flow pusher 91
    URL 192
    virtual networking filter 89
Flow Modification (FlowMod) 116
FlowER

about 194
    URL 194
Flowsim
    about 202, 203
    action 203
    datapath 203
    flow 203
    flow table 203
    group 203
    instruction 203
    match 203
    meter 203
    port 203
    queue 203
    references 203
FlowVisor API
    add-flowspace 164
    add-slice 164
    list-flowspace 164
    list-slice-info 164
    list-slices 164
    remove-flowspace 164
    remove-slice 164
    update-flowspace 164
    update-slice 164
    update-slice-password 164
FlowVisor slicing 166, 173
FlowVisor
    about 159, 201, 202
    references 160
FortNOX 207
Forwarding Abstraction Working Group (FAWG)
    218
Forwarding and Control Element Separation
    (ForCES) 18
    URL 76
Forwarding Information Base (FIB) 98, 204
forwarding model
    configure 216
    populate 216
Frenetic
    about 208
    accurate foundations 208
    high-level abstraction 208
    modularity 208

portability 208
URL 208

G

General Switch Management Protocol (GSMP) 17
Generalized Multiprotocol Label Switching
   (GMPLS) 221
Generic Routing Encapsulation (GRE) 93, 159,
   217
Glance 179

H

high availability (HA) 12
high-performance computing (HPC) 176
Higher Upper (HO) 222
Horizon 178

I

Indigo Virtual Switch (IVS) 45
Infrastructure as a Service (IaaS) 176, 199
Internet Control Message Protocol (ICMP) 59
Internet Engineering Task Force (IETF) 17
Internet of Things (IoT) 211
Intrusion Detection Systems (IDS) 12, 180
IP Address Management (IPAM) 187
isolation mechanism
  bandwidth isolation 160
  controller requests 162
  flow messages 161
  flowspace isolation 162
  internal state keeping 162
  OpenFlow control isolation 163
  slow-path packet forwarding 162
  Switch CPU isolation 161
  topology isolation 161

J

JavaScript Object Notation (JSON) 160

K

Kernel Virtual Machine (KVM) 158, 176
Keystone
  about 178
  authentication 179

credentials 179
endpoint 179
role 179
service 179
tenant 178
token 179
user 178

L

Link Layer Discovery Protocol (LLDP) 161, 215
Linux containers (LXC) 176
Lower Order (LO) 222

M

Maestro
  about 193
  URL 193
Mc-Nettle
  URL 74
Mininet
  about 49
  configuration, saving 67
  controller, configuring 64
  custom topology, creating on Mininet canvas 63
  experimenting 57
  flow table, monitoring 69
  host, configuring 66
  logs, generating 69
  MiniEdit 62
  MiniEdit preferences, setting 66
  Mininet GUI (MiniEdit), experimenting 61
  OpenFlow laboratory 47
  switch, configuring 65
  topology simulation, executing 69
  topology, creating 146, 152
  URL 49, 56, 61
mobile network applications 13
Multiprotocol Label Switching (MPLS) 93, 217,
  221

N

Nettle
  about 208
  URL 208
Network Address Translation (NAT) 102

network applications (Net Apps) 36, 73, 101, 121
Network Configuration Protocol (NETCONF) 18,
    93, 195
Network Development and Deployment Initiative
    (NDDI)
  about 209
  URL 209
network elements (NEs) 223
Network File System (NFS) 177
Network Function Virtualization (NFV)
  about 7, 13, 157, 199
  challenges 15
  FLOW_MATCH structure 165
  FlowVisor API 163
  isolation mechanism 160
  slice actions structure 166
  versus SDN 14
network management system (NMS) 220
Networking as a Service (NaaS) 179
Neutron plugins 183, 184, 185
Neutron
  about 176, 179
  URL 183
Node.js
  URL 85
NodeFlow
  about 85
  references 85
non-virtualized topology (NOX) 161
northbound 76
Northbound interface 36
Nova 180
NOX
  about 77
  URL 77

O

OF-PI
  goals 220
OFLIB-NODE 85
OFLIB-NODE libraries
  URL 85
OFlops 206
On-Demand Secure Circuits and Advance
    Reservation System (OSCARS) 207

Open Exchange Software Suite (OESS)
  about 209
  URL 209
Open Network Operating System (ONOS)
  about 189, 195
  distributed core 196
  northbound abstraction/API 196
  software modularity 197
  southbound abstraction/API 197
  URL 197
Open Networking Foundation (ONF)
  about 8, 217
  URL 18
Open Signaling (OPENSIG) 17
Open Virtualization Format (OVF) 49
Open vSwitch Database (OVSDB) 93
OpenContrail 199, 200
OpenDaylight (ODL)
  about 73, 92, 101, 110
  controller 110
  forwarding 132
  ODL-based SDN laboratory 113, 117
  URL 92, 110, 112
OpenFlow agent 223
OpenFlow enabled switches
  about 44
  hardware-based switches 46
  software-based switches 45
OpenFlow laboratory
  about 101, 105
  completing 106
  ethX, replacing 108
  external controllers 105
  with Mininet 47
OpenFlow Management and Configuration Protocol
    (OF-Config) 93
OpenFlow messages
  about 28
  asynchronous messages 34
  controller-to-switch 29
  symmetric messages 33
OpenFlow reference switch
  about 39
  asynchronous messages 43
  barrier 43

controller-Switch messages 41
flow table configuration 42
handshake 41
modify state 42
queue query 42
Read State (Statistics) 42
send packet 42
switch configuration 41
symmetric messages 44
OpenStack Networking (Neutron)
  URL 184
OpenStack Networking architecture
  about 180, 181, 182
  API network 183
  data network 183
  external network 183
  management network 183
OpenStack
  about 176
  Cinder 177
  Swift 177
Operations Support Systems (OSS) 13
Optical Core Network Resource Manager
  (OCNRM) 222
optical transport protocol extensions
  about 220
  Generalized Multiprotocol Label Switching 221
  Packet-optical Integration 222
Optical Transport Working Group (OTWG) 220
Organizationally Unique Identifier (OUI)
  URL 21

P

P4 components
  actions 216
  control programs 216
  headers 216
  parsers 216
  tables 216
packet forwarding
  about 212
  POF 212
  protocol-independent packet processors,
    programming 215
Packet-optical Integration (POI) 222

POFOX
  Communication 214
  Topology Discovery 214
POX
  about 77
  application, executing 78
Proposed Protocol-independent Layer 218
Protocol Oblivious Forwarding (POF)
  about 212
  architecture 212
  POFOX, structure 214
  POFSwitch 215
protocol-independent forwarding
  about 217
  OF-PI, objectives 220
  Table Type Patterns 218
  TTP and OF-PI, relationship 219
protocol-independent packet processors
  forwarding model, of P4 216
  P4 components 216
Python API of Mininet
  URL 102
Python
  URL 80

Q

Quality of Service (QoS) 42, 180, 209, 222

R

remote procedure call (RPC) 182
Representational State Transfer (REST) 179
RF-Controller (RF-C) 205
round trip time (RTT) 102
RouteFlow Client (RF-Client) 205
RouteFlow Proxy (RF-Proxy) 205
RouteFlow Server 205
RouteFlow
  about 204, 205
  URL 205
router
  address, configuring 149
  conclusion 151
  default gateway, configuring 150
  default gateway, configuring on host 147
  IP address, configuration on hosts 146

simulating, with Ryu controller 145
topology, creating on Mininet 146
verification 151
Routing Control Platform (RCP) 8
Ryu controller
starting 148
used, for simulating firewall 151
used, for simulating router 145
using, for switching hub 135, 138
Ryu
about 92, 195
application, executing 96
applications 95
architecture 93
controller 93
controller, installation 96
core processes 94
libaries 93
managers 94
northbound 94
OpenFlow protocol 93
URL 195

S

SANE/Ethane project
URL 18
SDN deployment
building blocks 18
SDN Hub starter VM kit 117
SDN/OpenFlow
activities 17
Secure Architecture for the Network Enterprise
(SANE) 8
Security, Scale, Stability and Performance (S3P)
92
Server Message Block (SMB) 177
Service Abstraction Layer (SAL) 110
service provider applications 12
software-based switches
about 45
indigo 45
LINC 46
Open vSwitch 45
Pantou (OpenWRT) 45
xorplus 46

Software-Defined Networking (SDN)
about 7, 46, 73, 101, 159, 175, 189
characteristics 8
use cases 11
Software-Defined Networking controllers 73
southbound 76
Spanning Tree Protocol (STP) 35, 42
special controllers 98
Subnetwork Access Protocol (SNAP) 21
switching hub
application, testing 141, 144
executing 139, 141
Ryu controller, using 135, 138
symmetric messages
echo message 33
error messages 34
experimenter 34
hello message 33

T

Table Type Patterns (TTP)
about 218
and OF-PI, relationship between 219
Technical Steering Committee (TSC) 92, 110
Topology Discovery 215
topology
creating, on Mininet 146, 152
Transaction Language 1 (TL1) 223
Transport Layer Security (TLS) 28
Travelping
URL 194
Trema
about 193
URL 194
Twister
about 207
URL 207
Type of Service (ToS) 21

U

use cases, SDN
campus networks applications 12
data center applications 11
mobile network applications 13
service provider applications 12

V

virtual ethernet (veth) 47
Virtual Extensible Local Area Network (VxLAN)
    159
Virtual Local Area Network (VLAN) 9

virtual machine (VM) 47, 179
virtual networking filter 89
Virtual Private Networks (VPN) 12

W

Web Server Gateway Interface (WSGI) 94